
SHE THRIVES

A HOLISTIC APPROACH TO WONE'S LIFE

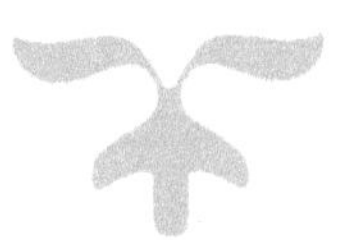

Index

Introduction

Welcome to a journey of holistic living tailored specifically for women—a path to vibrant health, deep fulfillment, and boundless joy. In a world that often pulls us in countless directions, where demands and distractions abound this book serves as a guiding light, illuminating the transformative power of holistic living. Here, we embark on a journey of self-discovery, where mind, body, and spirit unite in harmony to cultivate a life of purpose, passion, and profound well-being. Drawing upon ancient wisdom and modern science, we explore the interconnectedness of all aspects of our being, from nutrition and exercise to spirituality and self-care. Each page invites us to embrace our authentic selves, unleash our inner strength, and embark on a journey of empowerment, where every choice becomes an opportunity for growth and every challenge a stepping stone toward greater fulfillment. As we navigate this holistic odyssey together, let us embark with open hearts and curious minds, ready to awaken to our fullest potential and embrace the radiant vitality that awaits us.

Chapter 1

Introduction to Holistic Living for Women

1. Holistic living, and why is it important for women's well-being

Imagine a life where every aspect of your being—body, mind, and spirit—is nurtured and supported in harmony. That's the essence of holistic living, and it's a transformative journey that can profoundly impact your well-being as a woman. As you navigate the complexities of daily life, from managing relationships to pursuing your dreams, holistic living offers a holistic approach that acknowledges the interconnectedness of your emotions, physical health, and inner fulfillment.

The invisible weight that many of us carry. As a woman, you may find yourself facing with a range of emotions, from deep-seated traumas to everyday stressors. Holistic living recognizes the significance of emotional pain and provides a path towards healing and flexibility. Through practices such as meditation, mindfulness, and self-compassion, you can learn to honor your emotions, release past wounds, and cultivate a sense of inner peace and strength.

The tendency to prioritize others' needs over your own emotional pleasure. It's a pattern that many women struggle with, often at the expense of their own well-being. Holistic living empowers you to reclaim your emotional sovereignty and set boundaries that honor your needs and desires. By practicing self-care, assertive communication, and boundary-setting, you can cultivate a deeper sense of self-worth and fulfillment in your relationships and daily interactions.

So, where do you begin on your holistic living journey? Start by embracing self-awareness and self-compassion, acknowledging your emotions without judgment. Create an action plan that includes regular self-care practices such as journaling, meditation, or spending time in nature. Prioritize activities and relationships that nourish your soul and bring you joy, letting go of the need to please others at your own expense. Remember, holistic living is a journey of self-discovery and self-empowerment—a journey that honors your unique essence and celebrates your inherent worthiness.

2. How does holistic living differ from conventional approaches to health and wellness?

In conventional approaches, health and wellness often revolve around treating symptoms rather than addressing underlying causes, especially when it comes to emotional pain. You may find yourself seeking quick fixes like medication or short-term therapy sessions to alleviate distressing feelings. However, these methods may not fully address the root of your emotional struggles. Holistic living, in contrast, acknowledges emotional pain as a signal of deeper imbalance and encourages a more comprehensive exploration of your mind-body-spirit connection.

Moreover, conventional approaches may inadvertently perpetuate the "pleaser" point, urging you to prioritize others' needs over your own emotional well-being. You might feel pressure to constantly say yes to obligations and suppress your own desires to maintain harmony in relationships. Holistic living challenges this mindset by emphasizing the importance of self-care and setting boundaries that honor your emotional needs. It encourages you to prioritize actions that align with your authentic self and nurture your inner fulfillment.

So, what does this mean for you? It means embracing a personalized action plan rooted in holistic principles. Start by exploring mindfulness practices, such as meditation or journaling, to deepen your understanding of your emotions and thought patterns. Incorporate self-care rituals into your daily routine, whether it's taking a soothing bath, going for a nature walk, or indulging in a creative hobby. Practice assertive communication to express your needs and boundaries with clarity and compassion, fostering healthier relationships and a greater sense of empowerment in your life.

By embracing holistic living, you embark on a journey of self-discovery and self-empowerment that transcends conventional approaches. It's about nurturing your body, mind, and spirit in harmony, honoring your inherent worthiness, and embracing a life filled with vitality and purpose.

3. Key principles of holistic living that women can incorporate into their lives

Embrace the principle of self-awareness. Take time to tune into your thoughts, feelings, and sensations, without judgment or criticism. Recognize that emotional pain is a natural part of the human experience, and use it as an opportunity for self-reflection and growth. By cultivating self-awareness, you can gain insight into the root causes of your emotional struggles and develop strategies to address them holistically.

Prioritize self-care as a fundamental principle of holistic living. Understand that taking care of yourself is not selfish but essential for your overall well-being. Identify activities and practices that nourish your body, mind, and spirit, and make them a non-negotiable part of your daily routine. Whether it's practicing mindfulness, engaging in creative expression, or spending time in nature, prioritize actions that replenish your energy and nurture your inner fulfillment.

Setting boundaries that honor your emotional needs and desires. Recognize that it's okay to say no to commitments that drain your energy or compromise your well-being. Practice assertive communication to express your boundaries with clarity and compassion, both with yourself and others. By setting healthy boundaries, you create space for greater self-respect, autonomy, and authenticity in your relationships and daily interactions.

Cultivate a mindset of self-compassion as you navigate the ups and downs of your holistic living journey. Treat yourself with kindness and understanding, especially when facing challenges or setbacks. Practice self-compassionate self-talk and embrace your imperfections as part of what makes you uniquely human. Remember that healing emotional pain and releasing the "pleaser" point require patience, perseverance, and a whole lot of self-love.

Incorporating these key principles into your life can help you embrace holistic living as a transformative path to greater well-being and fulfillment. By prioritizing self-awareness, self-care, boundaries, and self-compassion, you empower yourself to navigate life's challenges with grace, resilience, and authenticity.

4. Holistic living empower women to take charge of their health and happiness?

Holistic living invites you to view yourself as a whole person—body, mind, and spirit—rather than focusing solely on individual aspects of your health. By embracing this holistic perspective, you recognize that your well-being is interconnected and multifaceted, allowing you to address root causes of issues rather than just treating symptoms. This approach empowers you to become an active participant in your health journey, making informed choices that support your overall vitality and happiness.

One interesting aspect of holistic living is its emphasis on prevention and proactive self-care. Rather than waiting until you're unwell to take action, holistic living encourages you to adopt habits and practices that promote wellness and resilience. This might include incorporating nourishing foods into your diet, engaging in regular physical activity that you enjoy, or practicing mindfulness techniques to manage stress. By taking a proactive approach to your health, you not only prevent illness but also enhance your overall quality of life.

Moreover, holistic living recognizes the importance of addressing emotional well-being as a key component of health and happiness. This means acknowledging and honoring your emotions, whether they're positive or negative, and developing healthy coping mechanisms to navigate life's challenges. By prioritizing self-awareness, self-compassion, and emotional resilience, you cultivate a deeper sense of inner peace and contentment that positively impacts every aspect of your life.

Holistic living empowers you to cultivate a sense of empowerment and autonomy over your own health and happiness. Rather than relying solely on external sources for validation or guidance, you learn to trust your intuition and inner wisdom to make decisions that align with your values and goals. This might involve setting boundaries in your relationships, advocating for your needs in healthcare settings, or pursuing activities and interests that bring you joy and fulfillment. By embracing your power to shape your own well-being, you become the architect of your own happiness, capable of creating a life that truly nourishes and sustains you.

Incorporating these unique and interesting aspects of holistic living into your life can empower you to take charge of your health and happiness in a way that's both fulfilling and sustainable. By embracing a holistic perspective, prioritizing prevention and proactive self-care, addressing emotional well-being, and cultivating a sense of empowerment, you can create a life that honors your inherent worthiness and supports your flourishing in every way.

5. Some common misconceptions about holistic living, and how can they be addressed?

One dominant misconception is that holistic living is solely focused on alternative or complementary therapies, such as acupuncture or herbal medicine, and dismisses conventional medical treatments. However, holistic living is about integrating the best of both worlds—embracing evidence-based practices while also recognizing the importance of holistic approaches that consider the whole person. By adopting a balanced approach to your health and well-being, you can benefit from a wide range of modalities that support your emotional, physical, and spiritual health.

Another misconception is that holistic living requires drastic lifestyle changes or adhering to strict dietary regimens. While making healthy choices is certainly a part of holistic living, it's not about perfection or deprivation. Instead, it's about cultivating mindfulness and balance in your daily life, making choices that align with your values and support your overall well-being. By taking a gradual and sustainable approach to holistic living, you can create lasting change that enhances your health and happiness without feeling overwhelmed or restricted.

Some may believe that holistic living is only for those who are already spiritually inclined or deeply committed to alternative practices. However, holistic living is inclusive and adaptable, meaning it can be tailored to meet your individual needs and beliefs. Whether you're interested in exploring mindfulness meditation, incorporating yoga into your routine, or simply prioritizing self-care and emotional well-being, there are endless ways to embrace holistic living that resonate with you personally.

There's a misconception that holistic living is a solitary journey, disconnected from the support and guidance of healthcare professionals or community resources. In reality, holistic living thrives on collaboration and connection, encouraging you to seek out support from a variety of sources, including therapists, nutritionists, support groups, and holistic practitioners. By building a network of support that aligns with your holistic goals, you can navigate emotional pain, release the "pleaser" point, and cultivate a life of greater health, happiness, and fulfillment.

In addressing these common misconceptions about holistic living, you empower yourself to embrace a more expansive and inclusive approach to well-being. By integrating evidence-based practices with holistic principles, adopting a balanced and sustainable approach, honoring your individual beliefs and needs, and seeking out supportive resources, you can embark on a holistic living journey that truly nourishes and sustains you in every way.

6. How does holistic living consider the interconnectedness of body, mind, and spirit in women's health?

Holistic living recognizes that your emotional well-being profoundly impacts your physical health and vice versa. When you experience emotional pain, whether it's from past traumas or daily stressors, it can manifest physically in the form of headaches, muscle tension, or digestive issues. Conversely, physical discomfort or illness can contribute to feelings of emotional distress. By addressing emotional pain holistically through practices like therapy, mindfulness, and self-compassion, you can support your overall well-being and enhance your body's ability to heal and thrive.

Moreover, holistic living acknowledges the "pleaser" point—the tendency to prioritize others' needs over your own emotional fulfillment—and its impact on women's health. When you consistently suppress your own desires or sacrifice your well-being to please others, it can lead to feelings of resentment, burnout, and disconnection from your authentic self. Holistic living empowers you to set boundaries, prioritize self-care, and honor your own needs and desires with compassion and intention. By releasing the "pleaser" point and embracing practices that nurture your spirit, you cultivate greater inner fulfillment and resilience.

Action plans are essential in holistic living, providing you with practical tools and strategies to support your holistic well-being. Consider creating a personalized action plan that encompasses daily self-care practices, such as mindfulness meditation, journaling, or engaging in creative expression. Set aside time each day to nurture your body, mind, and spirit, whether it's through movement, relaxation, or connecting with loved ones. By committing to your action plan with consistency and intention, you create a foundation for holistic living that supports your health and happiness in every aspect of your life.

In essence, holistic living embraces the interconnectedness of your body, mind, and spirit, recognizing that true well-being arises from nurturing all aspects of your being. By addressing emotional pain, releasing the "pleaser" point, and implementing actionable steps to support your holistic well-being, you empower yourself to take charge of your health and happiness in a way that honors your unique essence and celebrates your inherent worthiness.

7. Benefits of adopting a holistic approach to life for women of all ages

By embracing holistic practices, you unlock the power to transform emotional pain into profound growth and resilience. Imagine navigating life's twists and turns with a newfound sense of self-awareness and inner peace, armed with tools like therapy, mindfulness, and self-compassion to navigate even the stormiest seas of emotional turmoil. By honoring and addressing your emotional wounds, you embark on a journey of self-discovery and healing that propels you forward with newfound strength and clarity.

By releasing the "pleaser" point—the invisible force that compels you to put everyone else's needs before your own—you open the door to a world of authenticity and fulfillment in your relationships and daily interactions. Picture yourself setting boundaries with confidence, prioritizing self-care with unapologetic joy, and honoring your own needs and desires with unwavering determination. As you reclaim your power and autonomy, you cultivate deeper connections and a stronger sense of self-worth that radiates outwards, transforming your world from the inside out.

The secret sauce that turns dreams into reality. Imagine crafting a personalized action plan that's as unique as you are, filled with daily rituals and practices that nurture your body, mind, and spirit. From sunrise yoga sessions to moonlit journaling escapades, each action step brings you closer to a life that's bursting with vitality and purpose. By committing to your action plan with unwavering dedication and intention, you lay the foundation for holistic living that supports your health and happiness in every facet of your life.

So, are you ready to embark on this exhilarating journey of holistic living? By embracing emotional growth, releasing the "pleaser" point, and crafting actionable steps to support your holistic well-being, you unlock the door to a world of endless possibilities and boundless joy.

8. Integrate holistic practices into their daily routines and lifestyles

Consider starting your day with a mindful morning ritual, such as meditation, yoga, or deep breathing exercises. Dedicate a few minutes each morning to connect with your body, mind, and spirit, setting positive intentions for the day ahead. By incorporating these practices into your morning routine, you create a foundation of peace and clarity that sets the tone for a vibrant and fulfilling day.

Infuse your daily activities with moments of mindfulness and presence. Whether you're eating a meal, taking a walk, or engaging in household chores, bring your full attention to the present moment. Notice the sights, sounds, and sensations around you, and savor each experience with gratitude and awareness. By cultivating mindfulness in your daily life, you enhance your ability to stay grounded, centered, and connected to the beauty of the present moment.

Prioritizing self-care and relaxation. Set aside time each day to indulge in activities that nourish your body, mind, and spirit, whether it's reading a book, taking a bubble bath, or practicing a hobby you love. By honoring your need for rest and rejuvenation, you replenish your energy reserves and cultivate a deeper sense of inner peace and well-being.

Consider creating a holistic action plan that outlines specific practices and goals you'd like to incorporate into your daily routine. This could include setting aside time for exercise, meal planning and preparation, journaling, or connecting with loved ones. By breaking down your goals into manageable steps and scheduling them into your daily routine, you ensure that holistic practices become an integral part of your lifestyle, rather than just an afterthought.

In essence, integrating holistic practices into your daily routine and lifestyle empowers you to cultivate greater well-being, balance, and fulfillment in every aspect of your life. By starting your day with mindful rituals, infusing each moment with presence and gratitude, prioritizing self-care and relaxation, and creating a holistic action plan, you create a roadmap to vibrant living that honors your body, mind, and spirit in every way.

9. Resources and support are available for women interested in exploring holistic living further

Consider seeking out books, podcasts, and online resources that offer insights and guidance on holistic living. From inspirational memoirs to practical guides on mindfulness and self-care, there's a wealth of information available to support your journey. Look for resources that resonate with your interests and values, and explore topics such as meditation, nutrition, alternative therapies, and personal development. By immersing yourself in the wisdom of holistic living experts and thought leaders, you gain valuable insights and inspiration to guide your own path.

Consider connecting with like-minded individuals and communities who share your passion for holistic living. Whether it's joining a local yoga class, attending a wellness workshop, or participating in online forums and social media groups, surrounding yourself with supportive peers can be incredibly enriching and empowering. Seek out opportunities to share experiences, ask questions, and learn from others who are on a similar journey. By building a network of support, you create a sense of belonging and camaraderie that fuels your growth and evolution.

Working with holistic practitioners who can provide personalized guidance and support tailored to your unique needs and goals. From holistic health coaches and nutritionists to therapists and energy healers, there are many professionals who specialize in holistic approaches to well-being. Schedule consultations with practitioners who resonate with you, and explore how their expertise can complement your holistic living journey. By investing in professional support, you gain valuable insights, tools, and strategies to optimize your health and happiness.

The world is brimming with resources and support for women interested in exploring holistic living further. By immersing yourself in books, podcasts, and online resources, connecting with supportive communities, seeking guidance from holistic practitioners, and creating your own action plan, you embark on a transformative journey of self-discovery, empowerment, and well-being.

10. Embracing holistic living lead to greater fulfillment and balance in women's lives

Embracing holistic living opens a pathway to greater fulfillment and balance in your life, weaving together the threads of your physical, emotional, and spiritual well-being into a harmonious tapestry of vitality and joy. By prioritizing self-awareness and self-care, you cultivate a deeper understanding of your needs and desires, allowing you to make choices that align with your values and bring you true fulfillment. Consider starting your journey by setting aside time each day for practices like meditation, journaling, or movement that nurture your body, mind, and spirit, setting the stage for a life filled with purpose and passion.

Holistic living encourages you to release the "pleaser" point—the tendency to prioritize others' needs over your own emotional fulfillment—and reclaim your power and autonomy. By setting boundaries, practicing assertive communication, and honoring your own needs and desires with compassion and intention, you create space for greater authenticity and balance in your relationships and daily interactions. Take action by identifying areas of your life where you may be overextending yourself or sacrificing your well-being to please others, and commit to setting boundaries that honor your own needs and priorities.

Embracing holistic living fosters a sense of interconnectedness and wholeness, recognizing that your well-being is intimately linked to the well-being of those around you and the world at large. By nurturing your own body, mind, and spirit with compassion and intention, you cultivate a ripple effect of positivity and healing that extends outward into your relationships, your community, and the world. Consider exploring opportunities to give back, whether through volunteering, acts of kindness, or advocating for causes that resonate with you, amplifying the impact of your holistic living journey and fostering greater fulfillment and balance for all.

Embracing holistic living is a transformative journey of self-discovery, empowerment, and well-being that leads to greater fulfillment and balance in every aspect of your life. By prioritizing self-awareness and self-care, releasing the "pleaser" point, fostering interconnectedness and wholeness, and taking action to align your life with your values and goals, you create a life that honors your unique essence and celebrates your inherent worthiness.

Chapter 2

Nutrition for Women's Health

1. Nutritional needs specific to women, and how do they vary throughout the life stages

During adolescence, as your body undergoes rapid growth and development, it's essential to prioritize nutrient-dense foods that provide the building blocks for healthy bones, muscles, and organs. Focus on consuming adequate amounts of calcium, iron, and vitamin D to support bone health and prevent deficiencies. Incorporate foods such as dairy products, leafy greens, lean meats, and fortified cereals into your diet to meet these needs.

As you transition into adulthood and potentially enter your reproductive years, your nutritional needs may shift to support overall health and fertility. It's important to prioritize a balanced diet rich in essential nutrients, including folate, omega-3 fatty acids, and antioxidants, to support reproductive health and hormone balance. Incorporate foods such as fruits, vegetables, whole grains, fatty fish, and legumes into your diet to provide essential nutrients that support reproductive health and hormone balance. Additionally, consider incorporating lifestyle factors such as regular physical activity, stress management, and adequate sleep to support overall well-being during this stage of life.

During pregnancy and lactation, your nutritional needs increase significantly to support the growth and development of your baby. Focus on consuming nutrient-dense foods that provide essential vitamins and minerals, including folic acid, iron, calcium, and protein, to support fetal growth and development and ensure optimal health for both you and your baby. Incorporate foods such as lean meats, dairy products, leafy greens, whole grains, and legumes into your diet to meet these increased needs. Consider consulting with a healthcare professional or registered dietitian to develop a personalized nutrition plan that supports a healthy pregnancy and postpartum recovery.

As you transition into perimenopause and menopause, your nutritional needs may shift once again to support hormonal balance and overall health. Focus on consuming foods rich in phytoestrogens, such as soy products, flaxseeds, and legumes, to help alleviate symptoms of menopause such as hot flashes and night sweats. Additionally, prioritize foods rich in calcium and vitamin D to support bone health and reduce the risk of osteoporosis. Consider incorporating lifestyle factors such as regular exercise, stress management, and adequate sleep to support overall well-being during this stage of life.

In summary, understanding your specific nutritional needs throughout the various life stages empowers you to make informed choices that support your health and vitality at every age. By prioritizing nutrient-dense foods, incorporating lifestyle factors such as regular physical activity and stress management, and consulting with healthcare professionals or registered dietitians as needed, you can optimize your nutritional intake and support overall well-being throughout the journey of womanhood.

2. Diet support to hormonal balance, reproductive health, and overall well-being in women

Prioritizing a balanced diet rich in nutrient-dense foods can support hormonal balance by providing the essential vitamins, minerals, and antioxidants needed for optimal hormone production and regulation. Incorporate a variety of fruits, vegetables, whole grains, lean proteins, and healthy fats into your meals to ensure you're getting a wide range of nutrients that support hormonal health. Consider adding foods rich in omega-3 fatty acids, such as fatty fish, flaxseeds, and walnuts, which have been shown to support hormone production and reduce inflammation in the body.

Specific nutrients and dietary patterns have been linked to improved reproductive health in women. For example, consuming adequate amounts of folate, found in leafy greens, legumes, and fortified grains, can reduce the risk of neural tube defects during pregnancy and support fertility. Additionally, maintaining stable blood sugar levels through balanced meals and snacks can help regulate menstrual cycles and support reproductive function. Consider working with a healthcare professional or registered dietitian to develop a personalized nutrition plan that supports your reproductive health goals.

Hormonal balance and reproductive health, diet plays a crucial role in supporting overall well-being in women by providing the energy and nutrients needed for optimal physical and mental function. Prioritize whole, unprocessed foods and limit your intake of refined sugars, unhealthy fats, and processed foods, which can contribute to inflammation, hormonal imbalances, and mood swings.

Incorporate a variety of colorful fruits and vegetables, lean proteins, whole grains, and healthy fats into your meals to ensure you're meeting your nutritional needs and supporting your body's natural detoxification processes.

Incorporating lifestyle factors such as regular physical activity, stress management techniques, and adequate sleep into your daily routine to complement your dietary efforts and support overall well-being. Engage in activities that you enjoy, such as yoga, walking, or dancing, to promote physical and mental health. Practice stress-reducing techniques such as mindfulness meditation, deep breathing exercises, or spending time in nature to support hormone balance and reduce the impact of stress on your body. Aim for adequate sleep each night to support hormone regulation, energy levels, and overall vitality.

Prioritizing a balanced diet rich in nutrient-dense foods, supporting reproductive health through specific nutrients and dietary patterns, and complementing dietary efforts with lifestyle factors such as regular physical activity, stress management, and adequate sleep can support hormonal balance, reproductive health, and overall well-being in women. By taking proactive steps to optimize your diet and lifestyle, you empower yourself to thrive and flourish in every aspect of your life.

3. What are some nutrient-rich foods that women should prioritize in their diets, and why?

Incorporating leafy greens such as spinach, kale (cabbage), and fenugreek leaves into your meals on a regular basis. These powerhouse greens are packed with essential nutrients like vitamins A, C, and K, as well as folate, iron, and calcium, which support immune function, bone health, and overall vitality. Try adding a handful of leafy greens to smoothies, salads, stir-fries, or omelets to boost your nutrient intake and support your well-being.

Prioritize fatty fish such as salmon, mackerel, and sardines as a rich source of omega-3 fatty acids, which are essential for heart health, brain function, and inflammation reduction. Omega-3 fatty acids have been shown to support hormonal balance, reduce menstrual cramps, and alleviate symptoms of depression and anxiety in women. Aim to include fatty fish in your diet at least twice a week to reap the benefits of these essential nutrients for your overall health and well-being.

Incorporating a variety of colorful fruits and vegetables into your meals and snacks to provide a wide range of vitamins, minerals, and antioxidants that support immune function, cellular repair, and disease prevention. Berries such as strawberries, blueberries, and Indian gooseberries are particularly rich in antioxidants like vitamin C and flavonoids, which help protect against oxidative stress and inflammation in the body. Try adding a handful of berries to oatmeal, yogurt, or smoothie bowls for a delicious and nutritious boost of antioxidants.

Don't forget to include sources of lean protein such as poultry, eggs, tofu, paneer, and legumes in your diet to support muscle repair, hormone production, and satiety. Protein-rich foods are essential for maintaining muscle mass, supporting metabolic function, and regulating appetite and blood sugar levels. Incorporate a serving of lean protein into each meal and snack to help you feel satisfied and energized throughout the day.

Prioritizing nutrient-rich foods such as leafy greens, fatty fish, colorful fruits and vegetables, and lean protein sources can support optimal health and vitality in women. By incorporating these foods into your meals and snacks on a regular basis, you provide your body with the essential nutrients it needs to thrive and flourish in every aspect of your life. Consider creating a weekly meal plan that includes a variety of nutrient-rich foods to ensure you're meeting your nutritional needs and supporting your overall well-being.

4. Mindful eating practices help women develop a healthier relationship with food

Mindful eating invites you to tune into your body's hunger and fullness cues, allowing you to eat in response to physical hunger rather than emotional triggers or external cues. By practicing mindfulness during meals and snacks, you become more attuned to sensations of hunger, fullness, and satisfaction, helping you make informed choices that honor your body's needs and preferences. Try starting each meal with a few deep breaths and a moment of gratitude for the nourishment before you, setting the stage for a mindful eating experience that supports your well-being.

Moreover, mindful eating encourages you to slow down and savor each bite, allowing you to fully appreciate the flavors, textures, and aromas of your food. By eating more slowly and mindfully, you give yourself the opportunity to enjoy your meals and snacks more fully, leading to greater satisfaction and satiety. Consider putting away distractions such as phones, computers, and TVs during meal times, and focus on the sensory experience of eating, from the crunch of fresh vegetables to the aroma of a steaming bowl of soup.

Mindful eating fosters a non-judgmental attitude towards food and eating, freeing you from guilt, shame, and restrictive dieting behaviors. By approaching food with curiosity, compassion, and self-compassion, you cultivate a healthier relationship with food that's based on self-care and nourishment rather than rules or restrictions. Practice letting go of thoughts of "good" or "bad" foods, and instead focus on how different foods make you feel physically, emotionally, and mentally. By embracing a mindset of self-compassion and acceptance, you create space for greater freedom and joy in your relationship with food.

Incorporating mindful eating practices into your daily routine through simple action steps such as mindful meal planning, mindful grocery shopping, and mindful cooking. Take time to plan and prepare meals that nourish your body and satisfy your taste buds, incorporating a variety of colors, flavors, and textures into your diet. When grocery shopping, tune into your body's hunger and cravings, and choose foods that align with your nutritional needs and preferences. And when cooking, engage your senses fully, from the sight and smell of fresh ingredients to the sound of sizzling pans and bubbling pots.

In summary, practicing mindful eating can help you develop a healthier relationship with food by tuning into your body's hunger and fullness cues, savoring each bite, fostering a non-judgmental attitude towards food, and incorporating mindful eating practices into your daily routine. By embracing mindfulness during meals and snacks, you empower yourself to make informed choices that honor your body's needs and preferences, leading to greater satisfaction, well-being, and joy in your relationship with food.

5. Role of supplements and superfoods play in supporting women's nutritional needs

Supplements can serve as valuable tools to fill in nutritional gaps and support optimal health, especially when dietary intake may be insufficient or when specific nutrient needs are increased. For example, women may benefit from supplementing with iron to prevent anemia, calcium and vitamin D to support bone health, and omega-3 fatty acids to support heart health and brain function. Consider consulting with a healthcare professional or registered dietitian to assess your individual nutrient needs and determine if supplementation is appropriate for you.

Superfoods—nutrient-dense foods that are rich in vitamins, minerals, antioxidants, and other beneficial compounds—can play a key role in supporting women's nutritional needs and overall well-being. Examples of superfoods include berries, leafy greens, fatty fish, nuts and seeds, and whole grains, which provide a wide range of essential nutrients that support immune function, heart health, brain function, and more. Consider incorporating a variety of superfoods into your diet on a regular basis to maximize your nutrient intake and support your health goals.

Supplements and superfoods can complement a balanced diet rich in whole, unprocessed foods, providing additional support for optimal health and vitality. While it's important to prioritize nutrient-dense foods as the foundation of your diet, supplements and superfoods can serve as valuable additions to help you meet your nutritional needs and support your health goals. Consider creating a personalized nutrition plan that incorporates a variety of whole foods, supplements, and superfoods to ensure you're getting the nutrients you need to thrive.

Take proactive steps to ensure the quality and safety of any supplements or superfoods you choose to incorporate into your diet. Look for supplements that are third-party tested for purity and potency, and choose superfoods that are organic, non-GMO, and minimally processed whenever possible. By prioritizing high-quality supplements and superfoods, you can maximize their benefits and support your health and vitality in the most effective way.

Supplements and superfoods can play a valuable role in supporting women's nutritional needs and overall well-being, providing essential nutrients and beneficial compounds that support immune function, heart health, brain function, and more. By consulting with a healthcare professional or registered dietitian, incorporating a variety of nutrient-dense foods into your diet, and prioritizing high-quality supplements and superfoods, you empower yourself to optimize your health and vitality at every stage of life.

6. How can women address common dietary challenges such as cravings, emotional eating, and food sensitivities?

Cravings—those powerful urges that often lead us to reach for less-than-healthy food choices. One effective strategy is to practice mindful eating, tuning into your body's hunger and fullness cues and exploring the underlying reasons behind your cravings. Are you truly hungry, or are you seeking comfort, distraction, or stress relief? By bringing awareness to your cravings and identifying healthier alternatives that satisfy your needs, such as a piece of fruit instead of candy or a handful of nuts instead of chips, you can satisfy your cravings while nourishing your body with nutrient-rich foods.

Emotional eating—a common coping mechanism for dealing with stress, boredom, or difficult emotions. One helpful approach is to develop alternative coping strategies that soothe and support you without relying on food. This could include practicing deep breathing exercises, going for a walk in nature, journaling your thoughts and feelings, or engaging in a favorite hobby or activity. By cultivating a toolbox of healthy coping mechanisms, you can navigate emotions without turning to food for comfort, leading to greater emotional resilience and well-being.

Food sensitivities—reactions that your body may have to certain foods or ingredients, such as gluten, dairy, or soy. If you suspect you have food sensitivities, consider keeping a food journal to track your symptoms and identify potential triggers. You may also benefit from working with a healthcare professional or registered dietitian to conduct elimination diets or food sensitivity testing to pinpoint specific culprits. By identifying and eliminating trigger foods from your diet, you can alleviate symptoms such as bloating, digestive issues, and fatigue, and support your overall health and well-being.

The importance of self-compassion and patience as you navigate dietary challenges. Remember that change takes time, and setbacks are a natural part of the journey. Be gentle with yourself and celebrate your successes, no matter how small. Focus on progress, not perfection, and trust in your ability to overcome challenges and create a healthier relationship with food. By committing to your well-being and taking proactive steps to address dietary challenges, you empower yourself to cultivate a nourishing and balanced relationship with food that supports your health and happiness for years to come.

7. Practical tips for meal planning, grocery shopping, and cooking nutritious meals?

Setting aside time each week to create a meal plan that includes a variety of nutritious and delicious meals. Start by browsing recipes online, flipping through cookbooks, or brainstorming ideas based on your favorite ingredients and dietary preferences. Once you've chosen your recipes, make a list of all the ingredients you'll need and plan your meals accordingly. By creating a meal plan ahead of time, you can save time and stress during the week and ensure that you have all the necessary ingredients on hand to prepare healthy meals.

Grocery shopping—the cornerstone of successful meal planning and preparation. Before heading to the store, take inventory of your pantry, fridge, and freezer to see what ingredients you already have and what you need to buy. Make a detailed shopping list based on your meal plan and stick to it as you navigate the aisles of the grocery store. Consider shopping the perimeter of the store, where you'll find fresh produce, lean proteins, and whole grains, and avoid the inner aisles filled with processed foods and sugary snacks. By planning ahead and sticking to your shopping list, you can avoid impulse purchases and ensure that you're bringing home nutritious ingredients that support your health goals.

Practical tips for cooking nutritious meals that are delicious and satisfying. Consider batch cooking and meal prepping on the weekends to save time and ensure that you have healthy meals ready to go during the busy week ahead. Chop vegetables, cook grains and proteins, and portion out ingredients for easy assembly later on. Experiment with different cooking methods such as roasting, steaming, grilling, and sautéing to add variety and flavor to your meals. And don't be afraid to get creative in the kitchen—try new recipes, flavor combinations, and cooking techniques to keep things interesting and enjoyable. By making meal prep and cooking a fun and rewarding experience, you can cultivate a positive relationship with food and nourish your body with delicious and nutritious meals.

Importance of flexibility and adaptability when it comes to meal planning, grocery shopping, and cooking. Life can be unpredictable, and it's okay to deviate from your meal plan or make substitutions based on what's available and convenient. Be open to trying new foods and recipes, and don't be discouraged by occasional setbacks or challenges. By approaching meal planning and cooking with a sense of curiosity, creativity, and flexibility, you empower yourself to create a healthy and sustainable eating routine that supports your health and well-being in the long run.

8. Women can navigate cultural and societal influences on diet and body image in a holistic way

It's essential to cultivate self-awareness and critical thinking skills to recognize and challenge societal messages and cultural norms around diet and body image. Take time to reflect on your own beliefs, values, and experiences related to food, weight, and beauty standards, and consider how they may have been shaped by external influences. By becoming more mindful of the messages you internalize and questioning their validity, you can begin to cultivate a more empowered and authentic relationship with food and body.

Prioritize self-care practices that nourish your body, mind, and spirit and support your overall well-being. Engage in activities that promote self-love, such as mindfulness meditation, journaling, spending time in nature, or practicing gratitude (As I mentioned in previous chapter as well). Surround yourself with supportive friends, family members, and communities who celebrate diversity and embrace body positivity. By prioritizing self-care and surrounding yourself with positive influences, you create a protective buffer against harmful societal messages and cultivate a stronger sense of self-worth and confidence.

Practice intuitive eating—a mindful approach to food and eating that focuses on honoring your body's hunger and fullness cues, rather than external rules or restrictions. Tune into your body's signals of hunger, fullness, and satisfaction, and trust yourself to make choices that support your health and well-being. Reject diet culture's emphasis on external appearance and weight loss, and instead focus on nourishing your body with a balanced and varied diet that brings you joy and satisfaction. By embracing intuitive eating, you can break free from the cycle of dieting and deprivation and cultivate a more peaceful and harmonious relationship with food and body.

Taking action to challenge and change the cultural and societal norms that perpetuate harmful attitudes and behaviors around diet and body image. Advocate for greater diversity and inclusivity in media representations of beauty and challenge harmful stereotypes and stigmas related to weight, size, and appearance. Support organizations and initiatives that promote body positivity, health at every size, and self-acceptance for all. By actively participating in efforts to create a more inclusive and supportive society, you contribute to positive social change and empower women everywhere to embrace their bodies and live fully and authentically.

In summary, navigating cultural and societal influences on diet and body image in a holistic way requires self-awareness, self-care, intuitive eating, and advocacy for positive social change. By cultivating mindfulness, prioritizing self-care, practicing intuitive eating, and challenging harmful norms and stereotypes, you empower yourself to cultivate a positive relationship with food, body, and self that honors your unique essence and celebrates your inherent worthiness.

9. What are the potential pitfalls of popular diets, and how can women make informed choices about their nutrition?

Many popular diets promote restrictive eating patterns that can lead to nutrient deficiencies, disordered eating habits, and negative impacts on overall health and well-being. Diets that severely restrict certain food groups or macronutrients may deprive the body of essential nutrients, leading to imbalances and deficiencies over time. Additionally, restrictive diets can fuel feelings of guilt, shame, and failure when individuals inevitably struggle to adhere to rigid rules and restrictions. By recognizing the potential pitfalls of restrictive diets, you can approach dietary choices with a balanced and informed perspective that prioritizes nourishment and sustainability over quick-fix solutions.

Popular diets often rely on short-term results and promises of rapid weight loss, rather than focusing on long-term health and well-being. Many fad diets promote unrealistic expectations and unsustainable practices that can ultimately lead to weight cycling, yo-yo dieting, and negative impacts on metabolism and body composition. Instead of chasing quick fixes and temporary results, prioritize holistic approaches to nutrition that emphasize balance, moderation, and self-care. Focus on nourishing your body with whole, nutrient-dense foods that support your overall health and vitality, rather than chasing after elusive weight loss goals.

Popular diets may overlook individual differences and unique nutritional needs, promoting a one-size-fits-all approach to nutrition that fails to account for factors such as genetics, metabolism, lifestyle, and personal preferences. What works for one person may not necessarily work for another, and rigid adherence to a specific dietary protocol may disregard your body's unique signals and needs. Instead of blindly following dietary trends or recommendations, take a personalized approach to nutrition by listening to your body, experimenting with different foods and eating patterns, and seeking guidance from qualified healthcare professionals or registered dietitians who can help you develop a nutrition plan that's tailored to your individual needs and goals.

Empower yourself to make informed choices about your nutrition by educating yourself about the science behind food and dietary patterns, rather than relying on sensationalized headlines or anecdotal evidence. Take time to research and critically evaluate dietary claims and recommendations, considering the quality of the evidence, the credibility of the source, and how the information aligns with your own values and experiences. By approaching nutrition with a curious and discerning mindset, you can sift through the noise of dietary trends and fads and make choices that support your health and well-being in a balanced and sustainable way.

In summary, navigating popular diets requires a critical eye and a commitment to prioritizing long-term health and well-being over short-term results. By recognizing the potential pitfalls of restrictive eating patterns, focusing on holistic approaches to nutrition, taking a personalized approach to your dietary choices, and educating yourself about the science behind food and dietary patterns, you empower yourself to make informed choices that honor your body, mind, and spirit in every way.

10. How can women listen to their bodies and cultivate intuitive eating habits that support their holistic well-being?

It's essential to cultivate mindfulness and presence during meals and snacks, tuning into your body's hunger and fullness cues and honoring your natural appetite. Before eating, take a moment to check in with yourself and assess your level of hunger. Are you truly hungry, or are you seeking comfort, distraction, or emotional relief? Eat when you're physically hungry, and stop when you're comfortably full, regardless of external cues or portion sizes. By listening to your body's signals and respecting its needs, you can cultivate a more intuitive and harmonious relationship with food and eating.

Practice attunement to your body's cravings and preferences, allowing yourself to choose foods that truly satisfy and nourish you on a physical, emotional, and psychological level. Instead of labeling foods as "good" or "bad," tune into how different foods make you feel physically, emotionally, and mentally. Notice how certain foods energize and uplift you, while others may leave you feeling sluggish or unsatisfied. By honoring your body's cravings and preferences without judgment or restriction, you can cultivate a deeper sense of trust and connection with yourself and your innate wisdom.

Prioritize pleasure and enjoyment in your eating experiences, savoring each bite and sipping each sip with mindfulness and gratitude. Allow yourself to indulge in foods that bring you joy and satisfaction, whether it's a piece of dark chocolate, a bowl of veggies, or a refreshing fruit smoothie. By embracing the pleasure of eating and savoring the sensory experience of food, you can enhance your enjoyment of meals and snacks and foster a positive and fulfilling relationship with eating.

Practice self-compassion and forgiveness as you navigate the ups and downs of intuitive eating, recognizing that it's a journey rather than a destination. Be gentle with yourself when you experience setbacks or challenges, and remember that every eating experience is an opportunity to learn and grow. Celebrate your successes, no matter how small, and acknowledge the progress you've made towards cultivating a more intuitive and balanced relationship with food and eating. By embracing self-compassion and forgiveness, you create space for greater peace, joy, and well-being in your relationship with food and yourself.

In summary, cultivating intuitive eating habits involves cultivating mindfulness and presence, attuning to your body's cravings and preferences, prioritizing pleasure and enjoyment, and practicing self-compassion and forgiveness. By listening to your body's signals, honoring its needs and desires, and approaching eating with mindfulness and self-compassion, you can cultivate a more intuitive and harmonious relationship with food that supports your holistic well-being in every way.

Chapter 3

Physical Wellness and Exercise

1. Physical benefits of regular exercise for women, both in the short term and long term

In the short term, regular exercise offers immediate benefits such as increased energy levels, improved mood, and enhanced cognitive function. Engaging in physical activity releases endorphins, neurotransmitters in the brain that act as natural mood lifters, reducing feelings of stress, anxiety, and depression. Additionally, exercise promotes better blood circulation, delivering oxygen and nutrients to your cells and tissues more efficiently, resulting in a temporary boost in energy and vitality. By incorporating regular exercise into your daily routine, you can experience immediate improvements in mood, energy levels, and mental clarity, setting a positive tone for the day ahead.

Regular exercise contributes to a wide range of long-term physical benefits that support women's health and well-being over time. Consistent physical activity strengthens muscles and bones, reducing the risk of osteoporosis and age-related muscle loss, and improving overall strength, flexibility, and balance. Exercise also plays a crucial role in maintaining a healthy weight and reducing the risk of chronic diseases such as heart disease, diabetes, and certain types of cancer. By committing to regular exercise throughout your life, you can support your long-term health and vitality, enjoying greater independence, mobility, and quality of life as you age.

Regular exercise supports optimal cardiovascular health, reducing the risk of heart disease and stroke by improving heart function, lowering blood pressure, and promoting healthy cholesterol levels. Engaging in aerobic activities such as walking, jogging, cycling, or swimming strengthens the heart muscle, enhances circulation, and increases the efficiency of oxygen delivery to your body's tissues. By incorporating cardiovascular exercise into your weekly routine, you can reduce your risk of developing cardiovascular disease and enjoy a healthier, more resilient heart for years to come.

Regular exercise contributes to improved immune function, reducing the risk of illness and infection and supporting your body's ability to fight off pathogens and disease. Moderate-intensity exercise has been shown to boost the production of white blood cells, antibodies, and other immune system components, enhancing your body's ability to defend against viruses, bacteria, and other harmful invaders. By prioritizing regular physical activity as part of your holistic health regimen, you can strengthen your immune system, reduce the risk of illness, and enjoy greater resilience and vitality in the face of life's challenges.

In summary, regular exercise offers a wealth of physical benefits for women, both in the short term and long term, supporting overall health, vitality, and well-being at every stage of life. By incorporating regular physical activity into your daily routine, you can experience immediate improvements in mood, energy levels, and mental clarity, as well as long-term benefits such as improved muscle and bone strength, reduced risk of chronic disease, better cardiovascular health, and enhanced immune function.

Whether you're walking, jogging, cycling, swimming, dancing, or practicing yoga, find activities that you enjoy and make them a regular part of your lifestyle, prioritizing movement as an essential component of your holistic health and wellness plan.

2. Women overcome barriers to exercise and establish a sustainable fitness routine

Identify and address the specific barriers that may be preventing you from engaging in regular exercise, whether it's lack of time, motivation, confidence, or access to resources. Take time to reflect on your current lifestyle, commitments, and priorities, and consider how you can make room for exercise in your daily routine. Look for opportunities to incorporate physical activity into your day, such as taking the stairs instead of the elevator, walking or biking to work, or scheduling shorter, more frequent workout sessions that fit into your busy schedule.

Cultivate a positive mindset and self-belief by setting realistic goals, celebrating your progress, and embracing a growth mindset that views challenges as opportunities for learning and growth. Start by setting small, achievable goals that align with your interests, abilities, and priorities, such as walking for 30 minutes a day, trying a new fitness class each week, or gradually increasing the intensity and duration of your workouts over time. By breaking your goals down into manageable steps and celebrating your successes along the way, you can build confidence and momentum towards establishing a sustainable fitness routine that supports your long-term health and well-being.

Find activities that you enjoy and make exercise fun and enjoyable by exploring a variety of fitness options and experimenting with different activities until you find what works best for you. Whether it's dancing, hiking, swimming, yoga, or strength training, choose activities that align with your interests, preferences, and personality, and make them a regular part of your routine. Consider joining a fitness class, sports team, or online community to connect with like-minded individuals and stay motivated and accountable to your goals. By making exercise enjoyable and social, you can increase your likelihood of sticking with it over the long term and reap the physical, mental, and emotional benefits of regular physical activity.

Prioritize self-care and recovery by listening to your body, honoring its needs, and incorporating rest and relaxation into your fitness routine. Balance high-intensity workouts with lower-intensity activities, such as yoga, stretching, or meditation, to promote recovery, reduce the risk of injury, and prevent burnout. Pay attention to signs of fatigue, stress, or overtraining, and adjust your workouts and schedule accordingly to prioritize your health and well-being. By taking a holistic approach to fitness that includes rest, recovery, and self-care, you can establish a sustainable fitness routine that supports your overall health and vitality for years to come.

In summary, overcoming barriers to exercise and establishing a sustainable fitness routine requires a combination of self-awareness, goal setting, enjoyment, and self-care. By identifying and addressing barriers, setting realistic goals, finding activities you enjoy, and prioritizing self-care and recovery, you can create a fitness routine that fits seamlessly into your lifestyle and supports your long-term health and well-being. Remember that consistency is key, and every step you take towards prioritizing movement and physical activity brings you closer to a healthier, happier, and more vibrant life.

3. What types of exercise are most beneficial for women's health, and how often should they be performed?

Prioritize a combination of cardiovascular exercise, strength training, flexibility, and balance exercises to support women's health and vitality. Cardiovascular exercise, such as walking, jogging, cycling, or swimming, improves heart health, boosts mood, and increases endurance and stamina. Aim for at least 150 minutes of moderate-intensity aerobic activity or 75 minutes of vigorous-intensity aerobic activity per week, spread out over several days, to reap the benefits of cardiovascular exercise.

Incorporate strength training exercises into your fitness routine to build lean muscle mass, improve metabolism, and support bone health. Strength training activities, such as lifting weights, using resistance bands, or doing bodyweight exercises, should be performed at least two days per week, targeting all major muscle groups. Start with light weights and gradually increase the intensity and resistance as your strength and confidence grow.

Prioritize flexibility and balance exercises to improve mobility, reduce the risk of injury, and enhance overall physical function. Activities such as yoga, Pilates, or stretching routines can improve flexibility, balance, and coordination, promoting better posture and movement patterns. Aim to include flexibility and balance exercises in your routine at least two to three days per week, focusing on gentle stretching and stability exercises that target key muscle groups and improve joint mobility.

Listen to your body and adjust your exercise routine as needed to accommodate your individual needs, preferences, and goals. Pay attention to signs of fatigue, pain, or discomfort, and modify your workouts accordingly to prevent injury and promote recovery. Remember that rest and recovery are essential components of a balanced fitness routine, so be sure to include rest days and relaxation activities in your schedule to recharge and rejuvenate your body and mind.

In summary, prioritize a well-rounded exercise routine that includes cardiovascular exercise, strength training, flexibility, and balance exercises to support women's health and well-being. Aim for at least 150 minutes of moderate-intensity aerobic activity, two days of strength training, and regular flexibility and balance exercises each week to reap the full benefits of physical activity. Listen to your body, adjust your workouts as needed, and prioritize rest and recovery to maintain a sustainable fitness routine that supports your overall health and vitality for years to come.

4. How can women prevent injury and stay safe while exercising, particularly during pregnancy and postpartum?

It's essential to listen to your body and honor its changing needs and limitations during pregnancy and postpartum. Consult with your healthcare provider before starting or continuing an exercise program to ensure that it's safe for you and your baby. Focus on low-impact, pregnancy-safe exercises that support your changing body and reduce the risk of injury, such as walking, swimming, prenatal yoga, and gentle strength training. Pay attention to how you feel during exercise and modify movements as needed to accommodate any discomfort or physical changes.

Prioritize proper form and technique to reduce the risk of injury and maximize the effectiveness of your workouts. Engage your core muscles, maintain good posture, and use controlled movements to minimize strain on your joints and muscles. Avoid exercises that involve lying flat on your back or putting excessive pressure on your abdomen, especially in later stages of pregnancy. Choose pregnancy-safe modifications for common exercises, such as squats, lunges, and push-ups, to ensure that you're protecting your body and your baby while exercising.

Stay hydrated, fuel your body with nutritious foods, and take breaks as needed to rest and recover during workouts. Pregnancy and postpartum are times of increased physical demand and hormonal changes, so it's important to listen to your body's signals and prioritize self-care. Stay hydrated by drinking plenty of water before, during, and after exercise, and eat a balanced diet rich in fruits, vegetables, lean proteins, and whole grains to support your energy levels and recovery. Take breaks as needed to rest and recharge, and don't hesitate to modify or skip exercises that don't feel comfortable or safe for you.

Lastly, seek guidance from qualified fitness professionals or healthcare providers who specialize in prenatal and postnatal exercise to ensure that you're receiving personalized support and guidance throughout your journey. Consider working with a certified prenatal or postnatal fitness coach or attending prenatal or postnatal exercise classes designed specifically for pregnant and postpartum women. These professionals can provide expert guidance on safe and effective exercise techniques, help you navigate common pregnancy-related challenges, and support you in maintaining a healthy and active lifestyle throughout pregnancy and beyond.

In summary, prioritize your safety and well-being while exercising during pregnancy and postpartum by listening to your body, practicing proper form and technique, staying hydrated and well-nourished, and seeking guidance from qualified professionals. By taking proactive steps to prevent injury and stay safe during exercise, you can support your health and well-being throughout every stage of motherhood and enjoy the many benefits of staying active for both you and your baby.

5. Role does strength training play in women's fitness, and how can it be integrated into workouts

Strength training is essential for women's fitness as it offers a multitude of benefits, including increased muscle mass, improved metabolism, enhanced bone density, and reduced risk of injury. Contrary to common misconceptions, strength training doesn't necessarily result in bulky muscles;

instead, it helps create a lean, toned physique by promoting muscle definition and improving overall body composition. Additionally, strength training plays a crucial role in supporting daily activities and functional movements, such as lifting, carrying, and bending, allowing you to perform everyday tasks with greater ease and efficiency.

Integrating strength training into your workouts can be accomplished through a variety of exercises that target different muscle groups and movement patterns. Begin by selecting compound exercises that engage multiple muscle groups simultaneously, such as squats, deadlifts, lunges, push-ups, and rows, to maximize efficiency and effectiveness. Incorporate a mix of resistance training modalities, including free weights, resistance bands, machines, and bodyweight exercises, to keep your workouts varied and engaging. Aim to include strength training exercises in your routine at least two to three times per week, allowing for adequate rest and recovery between sessions.

Focus on progressive overload and gradual increases in resistance, volume, and intensity to continue challenging your muscles and stimulating growth and adaptation over time. Start with lighter weights and higher repetitions if you're new to strength training, gradually increasing the weight and decreasing the repetitions as your strength and confidence improve. Keep track of your progress by logging your workouts, tracking weights and repetitions, and periodically reassessing your goals and adjusting your training program accordingly. By progressively challenging your muscles and pushing past your comfort zone, you can continue to see improvements in strength, endurance, and overall fitness.

Prioritize proper form, technique, and safety during strength training to minimize the risk of injury and maximize the effectiveness of your workouts. Focus on maintaining good posture, engaging your core muscles, and using controlled, deliberate movements throughout each exercise. Start with lighter weights and master the proper technique before progressing to heavier loads. Consider working with a qualified fitness professional or personal trainer who can provide guidance on proper form, technique, and program design, ensuring that you're safely and effectively reaching your fitness goals.

In summary, strength training is a cornerstone of women's fitness, offering a wide range of benefits for overall health and well-being. By integrating strength training into your workouts through a variety of exercises, focusing on progressive overload and gradual increases in resistance, prioritizing proper form and safety, and seeking guidance from qualified professionals, you can build strength, confidence, and resilience that empowers you to thrive in all aspects of life.

6. Women can incorporate flexibility and mobility exercises into their routines to support joint health and flexibility?

Prioritize dynamic stretching and mobility exercises as part of your warm-up routine to prepare your muscles and joints for movement and reduce the risk of injury. Incorporate dynamic movements such as arm circles, leg swings, hip circles, and spinal twists to gently mobilize your joints and increase blood flow to your muscles. Focus on moving through a full range of motion with control and intention, paying attention to any areas of tightness or discomfort. By incorporating dynamic stretching into your warm-up, you can improve joint mobility, enhance flexibility, and optimize your performance during exercise.

Incorporate static stretching and flexibility exercises into your cool-down routine to help relax and lengthen your muscles, improve flexibility, and promote recovery. Hold each stretch for 20-30 seconds, focusing on the major muscle groups such as the hamstrings, quadriceps, calves, hips, chest, and shoulders. Breathe deeply and relax into each stretch, being mindful of any sensations of tension or discomfort. Incorporating static stretching into your cool-down routine can help reduce muscle soreness, improve flexibility, and promote relaxation and recovery after exercise.

Explore mind-body practices such as yoga, Pilates, and tai chi to enhance flexibility, mobility, and overall well-being. These holistic disciplines combine movement, breath work, and mindfulness to promote physical and mental balance, reduce stress, and improve flexibility and joint health. Consider attending a yoga class, joining a Pilates studio, or practicing tai chi in the comfort of your own home to experience the transformative benefits of these practices. By incorporating mind-body exercises into your routine, you can cultivate a deeper connection to your body, reduce tension and stiffness, and enhance overall flexibility and mobility.

Prioritize consistency and gradual progression in your flexibility and mobility training to see long-term results and improvements. Incorporate flexibility and mobility exercises into your routine at least two to three times per week, gradually increasing the duration and intensity of your stretches over time. Set realistic goals for improving flexibility and mobility in specific areas of your body, such as increasing hamstring flexibility or improving shoulder mobility, and track your progress over time. By committing to regular flexibility and mobility training and staying patient and consistent, you can gradually enhance joint health, improve flexibility, and move with greater ease and freedom in your daily life.

In summary, incorporating flexibility and mobility exercises into your routine is essential for supporting joint health, improving flexibility, and promoting overall well-being. By incorporating dynamic stretching into your warm-up, static stretching into your cool-down, exploring mind-body practices such as yoga and Pilates, and prioritizing consistency and gradual progression in your training, you can enhance joint mobility, improve flexibility, and move with greater ease and grace in all aspects of your life.

7. What are the mental and emotional benefits of physical activity for women, beyond just physical health?

Regular physical activity has been shown to be a powerful mood booster, helping to alleviate symptoms of stress, anxiety, and depression by releasing endorphins, neurotransmitters in the brain that act as natural mood lifters. Engaging in exercise promotes feelings of relaxation, well-being, and mental clarity, helping you to manage the daily challenges and pressures of life with greater ease and resilience. Consider incorporating activities such as brisk walking, jogging, cycling, or dancing into your routine to experience the mood-enhancing effects of physical activity and elevate your spirits.

Physical activity provides a valuable outlet for stress relief and emotional expression, allowing you to release pent-up tension and emotions in a healthy and constructive way. Whether it's pounding the pavement during a run, hitting the punching bag at a boxing class, or flowing through yoga poses on your mat, exercise offers a safe and cathartic space to channel your energy and emotions, promoting a sense of release, empowerment, and renewal. Consider incorporating activities that resonate with you and allow you to express yourself authentically, whether it's through movement, breath work, or mindful meditation, to harness the transformative power of physical activity for emotional well-being.

Regular physical activity fosters a sense of empowerment, self-confidence, and self-efficacy, as you challenge yourself, set and achieve goals, and overcome obstacles along the way. Engaging in exercise helps you to connect with your body, appreciate its strength and capabilities, and celebrate its achievements, fostering a positive and empowering relationship with yourself. Set realistic goals for yourself, whether it's completing a 5K race, mastering a new yoga pose, or increasing your strength and endurance in the gym, and celebrate your progress and accomplishments along the way. By embracing the journey of personal growth and self-discovery through physical activity, you can cultivate greater self-confidence, resilience, and self-belief in all areas of your life.

Physical activity provides valuable opportunities for social connection, community support, and camaraderie, as you engage in shared experiences and common interests with others. Whether it's joining a sports team, attending group fitness classes, or participating in outdoor activities with friends and family, exercise offers a powerful platform for building relationships, fostering a sense of belonging, and nurturing social connections. Prioritize opportunities for social interaction and community engagement through physical activity, whether it's joining a local running club, attending fitness events, or organizing active outings with loved ones, to cultivate meaningful connections and support networks that enrich your life and enhance your overall well-being.

In summary, physical activity offers a wealth of mental and emotional benefits for women, extending far beyond just physical health, empowering you to cultivate a resilient mind, a vibrant spirit, and a thriving sense of well-being. By embracing the mood-enhancing effects of exercise, finding healthy outlets for stress relief and emotional expression, fostering a sense of empowerment and self-confidence, and prioritizing opportunities for social connection and community support, you can harness the transformative power of physical activity to nourish your mind, body, and soul and live your best life.

8. How can women stay motivated to exercise, even when facing obstacles or setbacks?

Cultivate a strong sense of purpose and intrinsic motivation by connecting with your personal reasons for exercising and the benefits it brings to your life. Reflect on how regular physical activity makes you feel physically, mentally, and emotionally, and envision the positive impact it has on your overall health, happiness, and quality of life. Write down your goals, aspirations, and motivations for exercising, and revisit them regularly to reaffirm your commitment and stay focused on what truly matters to you.

Set realistic and achievable goals that inspire and challenge you, while also allowing for flexibility and adaptation in the face of obstacles or setbacks. Break your goals down into smaller, manageable steps and celebrate your progress and accomplishments along the way. Whether it's completing a certain number of workouts each week, improving your performance in a specific exercise or activity, or reaching a milestone event or achievement, set clear, measurable goals that align with your interests, abilities, and priorities, and track your progress over time to stay motivated and accountable.

Seek support and accountability from friends, family, or fitness buddies who share your goals and can cheer you on, offer encouragement, and help keep you motivated and accountable. Consider joining a fitness community, online group, or social network where you can connect with like-minded individuals, share your successes and challenges, and draw inspiration and support from others who are on a similar journey. By surrounding yourself with positive influences and a supportive network of friends and allies, you can stay motivated, inspired, and empowered to overcome obstacles and setbacks and continue making progress towards your fitness goals.

Embrace a growth mindset and view obstacles and setbacks as opportunities for learning, growth, and resilience. Instead of letting setbacks derail you or discourage you from pursuing your goals, reframe them as temporary setbacks or learning experiences that offer valuable insights and lessons for growth. Practice self-compassion and forgiveness when you encounter challenges, and focus on finding solutions, adapting your approach, and moving forward with renewed determination and resilience. By adopting a positive and resilient mindset, you can navigate obstacles and setbacks with grace and resilience, staying motivated and committed to your fitness journey no matter what challenges may arise.

In summary, staying motivated to exercise requires a combination of purpose, goal setting, support, and resilience. By connecting with your personal motivations, setting realistic goals, seeking support and accountability, and embracing a growth mindset, you can stay inspired, empowered, and committed to prioritizing physical activity and nurturing your health and well-being, even in the face of obstacles or setbacks. Remember that your journey is unique to you, and every step you take towards prioritizing movement and self-care brings you closer to a healthier, happier, and more vibrant life.

9. Holistic approaches to recovery and rest that support women's overall fitness and well-being?

Prioritize quality sleep as a cornerstone of holistic recovery and well-being, ensuring that you get enough rest each night to support optimal physical, mental, and emotional health. Aim for seven to nine hours of uninterrupted sleep per night, creating a calming bedtime routine and sleep-friendly environment to promote relaxation and deep rest. Consider incorporating soothing activities such as gentle stretching, meditation, or reading into your evening routine to wind down and prepare your body and mind for sleep. By prioritizing quality sleep, you can enhance recovery, support hormonal balance, and improve overall health and vitality.

Embrace restorative movement practices such as yoga, gentle stretching, or restorative exercise classes to promote recovery, reduce muscle tension, and enhance flexibility and mobility. Incorporate these activities into your routine on rest days or as part of your cool-down after more intense workouts, allowing your body to recover and rejuvenate. Focus on gentle, mindful movement that encourages relaxation, deep breathing, and a sense of inner calm, promoting physical and mental balance and well-being.

Prioritize relaxation techniques such as deep breathing, meditation, or progressive muscle relaxation to reduce stress, promote relaxation, and support overall well-being. Set aside time each day to engage in mindfulness practices that encourage present-moment awareness and cultivate a sense of inner peace and calmness. Consider incorporating relaxation techniques into your morning routine, midday break, or evening wind-down to manage stress, reduce tension, and promote a greater sense of calm and equilibrium in your daily life.

Nourish your body with nutrient-dense foods, hydrate with plenty of water, and prioritize self-care practices such as massage, aromatherapy, or warm baths to promote physical and emotional healing and rejuvenation. Pay attention to your body's signals and honor its need for rest, recovery, and replenishment, listening to what it needs and providing the care and nourishment it deserves. By prioritizing holistic approaches to recovery and rest, you can support your overall fitness and well-being, enhance your resilience and vitality, and cultivate a deeper sense of balance and harmony in your life.

In summary, holistic approaches to recovery and rest are essential for supporting women's overall fitness and well-being, empowering you to prioritize restorative practices that nourish your body, mind, and spirit. By prioritizing quality sleep, embracing restorative movement practices, incorporating relaxation techniques into your daily routine, and nourishing your body with self-care practices, you can promote optimal recovery, reduce stress, and enhance your overall health and vitality. Remember that self-care is an essential part of any holistic fitness regimen, and by honoring your body's need for rest, recovery, and rejuvenation, you can support your well-being and thrive in all areas of your life.

10. Women can cultivate a positive body image and embrace their physical strength and capabilities through exercise?

Focus on shifting your mindset from appearance-based goals to goals that emphasize strength, function, and overall well-being. Instead of striving for a certain dress size or number on the scale, set intentions and goals that celebrate your physical abilities, such as improving strength, endurance, flexibility, or athletic performance. By shifting your focus to what your body can do rather than how it looks, you can cultivate a deeper appreciation for your physical capabilities and celebrate the unique strengths and abilities that make you who you are.

Surround yourself with positive influences and supportive communities that celebrate diversity, inclusivity, and body positivity within the fitness realm. Seek out fitness professionals, trainers, or influencers who promote a balanced and inclusive approach to health and wellness, prioritizing strength, function, and overall well-being over unrealistic ideals or standards. Engage with social media accounts, online communities, or local groups that celebrate body diversity, share empowering messages, and promote a healthy and positive relationship with exercise and fitness.

Choose exercise modalities and activities that align with your interests, preferences, and values, allowing you to engage in physical activity in a way that feels enjoyable, empowering, and authentic to you. Whether it's dancing, hiking, strength training, yoga, or team sports, find activities that bring you joy, challenge you, and allow you to connect with your body in a positive and empowering way. Set aside time each week to engage in activities that make you feel strong, capable, and empowered, and prioritize self-care and self-compassion throughout your fitness journey.

Practice self-compassion, gratitude, and mindfulness as you navigate your fitness journey, acknowledging and appreciating your body's strengths, capabilities, and resilience. Celebrate your progress and accomplishments, no matter how small, and cultivate a sense of gratitude for your body and all that it allows you to do each day. Practice mindfulness and presence during your workouts, focusing on how your body feels, moves, and responds to exercise, rather than getting caught up in negative self-talk or comparison. By cultivating a positive and empowered mindset, embracing your physical strength and capabilities, and celebrating your body for all that it is, you can foster a healthy and positive body image that empowers you to thrive in all aspects of your life.

Chapter 4

Mental and Emotional Well-Being

1. **Common stressors that women face in today's society, and how can they impact mental and emotional health**

Pressures of balancing multiple roles and responsibilities, such as work, family, caregiving, and social obligations, can create significant stress for women. Juggling the demands of career advancement, household management, childcare, and personal relationships can lead to feelings of overwhelm, burnout, and exhaustion, impacting mental and emotional well-being. It's essential to prioritize self-care, set boundaries, and delegate tasks when possible to manage stress and prevent feelings of being stretched too thin.

Societal expectations and gender norms can contribute to stress and anxiety for women, as they navigate cultural standards of beauty, success, and achievement. The pressure to conform to unrealistic standards of appearance, success, and perfectionism can lead to feelings of inadequacy, self-doubt, and low self-esteem, impacting mental and emotional health. It's important to challenge societal expectations and embrace a more compassionate and accepting attitude towards oneself, focusing on self-love, self-acceptance, and authenticity rather than external validation.

Experiences of discrimination, sexism, and gender-based violence can have a profound impact on women's mental and emotional health, leading to feelings of fear, anger, and powerlessness. Women may face discrimination in the workplace, educational settings, healthcare system, or within their personal relationships, contributing to stress, anxiety, and trauma. It's crucial to seek support from trusted friends, family members, or mental health professionals, and to advocate for yourself and others in the face of injustice or discrimination.

Challenges of navigating life transitions, such as pregnancy, motherhood, menopause, or aging, can create additional stress for women as they adjust to changes in their bodies, identities, and roles. Hormonal fluctuations, physical changes, and societal expectations surrounding these life stages can impact mental and emotional well-being, leading to feelings of uncertainty, isolation, and vulnerability. It's important to seek support from healthcare providers, therapists, or support groups, and to prioritize self-care, self-compassion, and resilience during times of transition and change.

In summary, women face a myriad of stressors in today's society, ranging from the pressures of balancing multiple roles and responsibilities to societal expectations, discrimination, and life transitions. These stressors can have a significant impact on mental and emotional health, leading to feelings of overwhelm, low self-esteem, anxiety, and trauma. It's essential to recognize and address these challenges proactively, prioritizing self-care, setting boundaries, seeking support, and challenging societal norms and expectations that contribute to stress and anxiety. By prioritizing mental and emotional well-being and advocating for yourself and others, you can navigate life's challenges with greater resilience, strength, and empowerment.

2. How does stress affect women differently than men, and what are some effective coping strategies?

Women may experience stress differently than men due to various factors, including hormonal fluctuations, societal expectations, and coping mechanisms. Hormonal changes throughout the menstrual cycle, pregnancy, postpartum period, and menopause can influence women's susceptibility to stress and anxiety, leading to fluctuations in mood, energy levels, and resilience. Moreover, societal expectations and gender roles may place additional pressure on women to prioritize caregiving, nurturing, and emotional labor, leading to feelings of overwhelm and burnout. Understanding these unique stressors can help women develop tailored coping strategies to manage stress effectively.

Women may be more likely to use social support and connection as coping mechanisms in response to stress, seeking comfort and reassurance from friends, family members, or support networks. Building strong social connections and cultivating a supportive network of friends and allies can provide a valuable source of emotional support, validation, and resilience during times of stress. It's essential to nurture relationships, prioritize meaningful connections, and reach out for support when needed, fostering a sense of belonging and community that buffers against the negative effects of stress.

Incorporating stress-reducing practices such as mindfulness, meditation, deep breathing, or yoga into daily life can help women manage stress and promote emotional well-being. Mindfulness-based techniques encourage present-moment awareness and non-judgmental acceptance of thoughts, feelings, and sensations, reducing reactivity and promoting a sense of calm and equanimity. By incorporating mindfulness practices into your routine, you can cultivate greater resilience, self-awareness, and emotional regulation, empowering you to navigate stress with grace and ease.

Prioritizing self-care and holistic well-being is essential for managing stress and promoting overall health and vitality. Engaging in activities that nourish your body, mind, and spirit, such as exercise, nature walks, creative expression, or relaxation techniques, can help alleviate stress and promote a sense of balance and well-being. Set aside time each day for self-care activities that bring you joy, relaxation, and fulfillment, and prioritize your needs and well-being as a central focus of your daily life. By prioritizing self-care and holistic well-being, you can cultivate resilience, strengthen your coping mechanisms, and navigate stress with grace and resilience.

In summary, women may experience stress differently than men due to hormonal fluctuations, societal expectations, and coping mechanisms, but there are effective strategies for managing its impact on mental and emotional well-being. By understanding the unique stressors that women face and implementing tailored coping strategies such as seeking social support, practicing mindfulness, prioritizing self-care, and fostering holistic well-being, you can navigate stress with resilience, strength, and self-compassion, empowering you to thrive in all aspects of your life.

3. Mindfulness play an important role in promoting mental and emotional well-being for women

Mindfulness offers a powerful tool for managing stress, anxiety, and overwhelm by encouraging present-moment awareness and non-judgmental acceptance of thoughts, feelings, and sensations. By practicing mindfulness techniques such as deep breathing, body scans, or mindful meditation, you can develop greater self-awareness and emotional regulation, reducing reactivity and promoting a sense of calm and equanimity in the face of life's challenges. Consider incorporating mindfulness practices into your daily routine, setting aside time each day for meditation, mindful movement, or reflection to cultivate a greater sense of inner peace and balance.

Mindfulness can help women navigate the complex and often overwhelming emotions that arise in response to life's ups and downs. By tuning into your thoughts, feelings, and bodily sensations with curiosity and compassion, you can develop greater emotional intelligence and resilience, allowing you to respond to difficult emotions with greater clarity, insight, and self-compassion. Practice self-compassion and kindness towards yourself as you navigate challenging emotions, recognizing that it's natural to experience a range of feelings and that you have the strength and resources within you to cope with whatever arises.

Mindfulness can support women in cultivating more meaningful and fulfilling relationships with themselves and others, fostering greater connection, empathy, and understanding. By practicing present-moment awareness and deep listening, you can cultivate deeper connections with yourself, allowing you to tune into your inner wisdom, intuition, and desires. Similarly, mindfulness can enhance your ability to empathize and connect with others, fostering more authentic and fulfilling relationships based on mutual respect, understanding, and compassion. Consider incorporating mindfulness practices into your interactions with yourself and others, cultivating greater presence and connection in your relationships and enhancing your overall well-being.

Mindfulness offers a pathway to greater self-discovery, personal growth, and spiritual fulfillment, allowing women to connect with their innermost selves and cultivate a sense of purpose, meaning, and fulfillment in life. By practicing mindfulness, you can tap into your innate wisdom and intuition, aligning with your values, passions, and aspirations. Set aside time for self-reflection, journaling, or contemplative practices to explore your inner landscape and deepen your connection to yourself and the world around you. By embracing mindfulness as a pathway to self-discovery and personal growth, you can cultivate greater resilience, authenticity, and fulfillment in all aspects of your life.

In summary, mindfulness offers a powerful pathway to promoting mental and emotional well-being for women, empowering you to cultivate greater awareness, resilience, and inner peace in your daily life. By incorporating mindfulness practices into your routine, navigating challenging emotions with compassion and clarity, fostering meaningful connections with yourself and others, and embracing mindfulness as a tool for self-discovery and personal growth, you can cultivate a deeper sense of well-being and fulfillment in all aspects of your life.

4. How can women cultivate resilience and emotional intelligence to navigate life's challenges?

Cultivate resilience by reframing challenges as opportunities for growth and learning, rather than insurmountable obstacles. Embrace a growth mindset that views setbacks and failures as valuable lessons that can strengthen your resilience and deepen your understanding of yourself and the world around you. Practice self-compassion and forgiveness when you encounter difficulties, recognizing that it's natural to experience setbacks and setbacks, and that each challenge you face offers an opportunity for personal growth and transformation. Set aside time for self-reflection and journaling to explore your thoughts, feelings, and experiences, and identify lessons learned and areas for growth.

Develop emotional intelligence by cultivating self-awareness, self-regulation, and empathy, empowering you to navigate difficult emotions with grace and compassion. Tune into your thoughts, feelings, and bodily sensations with curiosity and non-judgmental awareness, allowing yourself to fully experience and acknowledge your emotions without getting swept away by them. Practice self-regulation techniques such as deep breathing, progressive muscle relaxation, or mindfulness meditation to calm the nervous system and promote emotional balance and well-being. Additionally, cultivate empathy and understanding towards yourself and others, recognizing that everyone is facing their own struggles and challenges, and offering support and kindness wherever possible.

Build a strong support network of friends, family members, or mentors who can provide guidance, encouragement, and perspective during difficult times. Surround yourself with people who uplift and inspire you, offering a sense of belonging, validation, and understanding when you need it most. Reach out for support and connection when you're feeling overwhelmed or struggling, and be open to receiving help and support from others. Consider joining a support group, attending therapy or counseling sessions, or seeking guidance from a trusted mentor or advisor to help you navigate life's challenges with greater resilience and emotional intelligence.

Prioritize self-care and well-being as essential components of resilience and emotional intelligence, nurturing your body, mind, and spirit with practices that promote balance, vitality, and inner peace. Set aside time each day for activities that bring you joy, relaxation, and fulfillment, whether it's spending time in nature, engaging in creative expression, or practicing self-care rituals such as massage, aromatherapy, or warm baths. Nourish your body with nutrient-rich foods, prioritize regular exercise and movement, and ensure you get enough rest and sleep to support your physical and emotional well-being. By prioritizing self-care and well-being, you can build a solid foundation of resilience and emotional intelligence, empowering you to navigate life's challenges with grace, strength, and wisdom.

In summary, cultivating resilience and emotional intelligence is essential for navigating life's challenges with grace, strength, and wisdom. By reframing challenges as opportunities for growth, developing emotional awareness and regulation skills, building a strong support network, and prioritizing self-care and well-being, you can cultivate the resilience and emotional intelligence needed to thrive in the face of adversity. Remember that resilience is a skill that can be developed and strengthened over time, and by embracing challenges as opportunities for growth and learning, you can navigate life's ups and downs with greater confidence, courage, and resilience.

5. Some practical techniques for managing anxiety, depression, and other mental health concerns holistically

Prioritize self-care practices that nourish your body, mind, and spirit, promoting balance and vitality from a holistic perspective. Engage in activities that promote relaxation, such as mindfulness meditation, deep breathing exercises, or progressive muscle relaxation, to calm the nervous system and reduce symptoms of anxiety and depression. Set aside time each day for activities that bring you joy. By prioritizing self-care and well-being, you can cultivate a greater sense of balance and resilience, supporting your mental and emotional health in the process.

Cultivate healthy lifestyle habits that support optimal mental and emotional well-being, such as regular exercise, balanced nutrition, adequate sleep, and stress management techniques. Engage in activities that promote physical activity and movement, such as walking, jogging, yoga, or dance, to release endorphins and promote feelings of well-being and vitality. Nourish your body with nutrient-rich foods that support brain health and mood regulation, such as fruits, vegetables, whole grains, lean proteins, and healthy fats. Prioritize rest and relaxation by establishing a regular sleep routine and practicing relaxation techniques to promote restful sleep and reduce symptoms of anxiety and depression.

Seek support from trusted friends, family members, or mental health professionals who can provide guidance, encouragement, and perspective during difficult times. Reach out for support and connection when you're feeling overwhelmed or struggling, and be open to receiving help and support from others. Consider joining a support group, attending therapy or counseling sessions, or seeking guidance from a holistic healthcare practitioner who can provide personalized support and guidance tailored to your individual needs. By building a strong support network and seeking help when needed, you can navigate mental health concerns with greater resilience and empowerment.

Incorporate holistic healing modalities into your self-care routine, such as acupuncture, massage, energy healing, or herbal medicine, to support your mental and emotional well-being from a holistic perspective. Explore alternative therapies and complementary practices that resonate with you and align with your values and beliefs, and be open to trying new approaches to support your mental health and well-being. By taking a holistic approach to managing anxiety, depression, and other mental health concerns, you can cultivate greater resilience, empowerment, and well-being in your life, supporting your journey towards greater health and happiness.

6. Holistic approaches such as meditation, breathing technique, and visualization support women's mental and emotional health?

Meditation offers a powerful tool for calming the mind, reducing stress, and promoting inner peace and relaxation. By practicing mindfulness meditation, you can cultivate present-moment awareness and non-judgmental acceptance of thoughts, feelings, and sensations, reducing reactivity and promoting a sense of calm and equanimity. Set aside time each day for meditation practice, whether it's a short mindfulness session in the morning or evening, or a longer guided meditation session during breaks or downtime. By incorporating meditation into your routine, you can cultivate greater mental clarity, emotional balance, and resilience in the face of life's challenges.

Breathing techniques offer a simple yet effective way to regulate the nervous system, promote relaxation, and reduce symptoms of anxiety and stress. By practicing deep breathing exercises such as diaphragmatic breathing, box breathing, or alternate nostril breathing, you can activate the body's relaxation response, calm the mind, and promote a greater sense of well-being. Set aside a few minutes each day to practice deep breathing exercises, focusing on slow, deep breaths that expand the belly and chest and exhaling fully to release tension and stress. By incorporating breathing techniques into your daily routine, you can cultivate greater emotional resilience, reduce anxiety, and enhance your overall mental and emotional well-being.

Visualization techniques offer a powerful tool for harnessing the mind-body connection to promote healing, relaxation, and positive change. By engaging in guided visualization exercises, you can create mental images or scenarios that evoke feelings of peace, safety, and well-being, reducing stress and promoting emotional balance. Set aside time each day for visualization practice, whether it's imagining yourself in a peaceful natural setting, visualizing yourself accomplishing your goals and aspirations, or picturing yourself surrounded by love and support. By incorporating visualization techniques into your routine, you can tap into the power of your imagination to cultivate greater mental and emotional resilience, enhance your mood, and support your overall well-being.

Combining meditation, breathing techniques, and visualization into a holistic self-care routine that supports your mental and emotional health from multiple angles. Experiment with different techniques and practices to see what resonates with you and fits into your lifestyle, and be open to exploring new approaches as you navigate your journey towards greater well-being. Set aside dedicated time each day for your holistic self-care practice, prioritizing your mental and emotional health and well-being as a central focus of your daily routine. By incorporating meditation, breathing techniques, and visualization into your self-care routine, you can cultivate greater resilience, inner peace, and emotional balance, empowering you to thrive in all aspects of your life as a woman.

7. Benefits of seeking professional support, such as therapy or counseling, as part of holistic self-care

Professional therapy or counseling offers a safe and supportive space to explore and address mental and emotional challenges in a confidential and non-judgmental setting. A trained therapist or counselor can provide guidance, perspective, and support as you navigate difficult emotions, experiences, and life transitions, offering valuable insights and coping strategies to help you cope more effectively with stress, anxiety, depression, and other mental health concerns. Consider reaching out to a licensed therapist or counselor who specializes in holistic approaches to mental health and well-being, and who shares your values and beliefs regarding holistic healing and self-care.

Therapy or counseling can help you gain deeper self-awareness and insight into your thoughts, feelings, and behaviors, empowering you to make positive changes and cultivate greater self-compassion, resilience, and personal growth. Through self-exploration and reflection, you can uncover underlying patterns and beliefs that may be contributing to your mental and emotional challenges, gaining clarity and understanding that can support healing and transformation. Set aside dedicated time each week for therapy or counseling sessions, prioritizing your mental and emotional well-being as an essential aspect of your holistic self-care routine.

Professional support can provide you with valuable tools, techniques, and strategies to manage stress, anxiety, depression, and other mental health concerns more effectively, empowering you to build resilience, cope with challenges, and enhance your overall well-being. A skilled therapist or counselor can teach you evidence-based techniques to help you regulate emotions, challenge negative thinking patterns, and develop healthier coping mechanisms. Practice these techniques regularly outside of therapy sessions, incorporating them into your daily routine to support your mental and emotional well-being on an ongoing basis.

Seeking professional support can offer you a sense of validation and empowerment as you navigate your mental and emotional health journey, reminding you that you're not alone and that it's okay to ask for help when you need it. By investing in your mental and emotional well-being through therapy or counseling, you're demonstrating self-compassion and self-respect, prioritizing your needs and well-being as a central focus of your holistic self-care routine. Remember that seeking professional support is a courageous and empowering step towards greater healing, growth, and resilience, and that you deserve to receive the support and guidance you need to thrive in all aspects of your life as a woman.

8. **Women can create a supportive environment and cultivate healthy relationships that contribute to their emotional well-being**

Prioritize open and honest communication in your relationships, fostering trust, understanding, and connection with those around you. Take the time to express your thoughts, feelings, and needs authentically and assertively, while also listening actively and empathetically to the perspectives of others. Practice active listening techniques such as reflective listening, paraphrasing, and validation to ensure that you understand and validate the experiences and emotions of those you care about. Set aside dedicated time each week for meaningful conversations with loved ones, prioritizing quality time and connection as essential components of your relationships.

Establish healthy boundaries in your relationships, honoring your needs, preferences, and limits while also respecting the boundaries of others. Communicate your boundaries clearly and assertively, and be willing to enforce them when necessary to protect your emotional well-being and autonomy. Practice self-care and self-compassion as you navigate your relationships, prioritizing your needs and well-being as a central focus of your interactions. Set aside time each day for activities that nourish your body, mind, and spirit, whether it's practicing mindfulness, engaging in creative expression, or spending time in nature, and honor your boundaries by saying no to activities or commitments that drain your energy or compromise your well-being.

Cultivate a supportive network of friends, family members, and mentors who uplift and inspire you, offering a sense of belonging, validation, and understanding when you need it most. Surround yourself with people who share your values, goals, and interests, and who encourage you to grow, evolve, and thrive in all aspects of your life. Invest time and energy in nurturing your relationships, prioritizing quality time, shared experiences, and mutual support as essential components of your social network. Set aside time each week for social activities and gatherings, whether it's meeting friends for coffee, attending a community event, or participating in a hobby or interest group, and prioritize connection and community as vital aspects of your emotional well-being.

Practice forgiveness, compassion, and acceptance in your relationships, recognizing that everyone makes mistakes and has their own struggles and challenges. Cultivate empathy and understanding towards yourself and others, allowing for imperfections, vulnerabilities, and growth in your interactions. Let go of resentments, grudges, and judgments, and instead focus on fostering compassion, kindness, and connection in your relationships. Set aside time each day for self-reflection and gratitude, acknowledging the blessings and lessons that your relationships bring into your life, and cultivating a sense of appreciation and love for yourself and those around you. By creating a supportive environment and cultivating healthy relationships, you can enhance your emotional well-being, cultivate greater resilience and fulfillment, and thrive in your personal and interpersonal connections as a woman.

9. What role does self-compassion play in women's holistic health, and how can it be cultivated?

Self-compassion is a cornerstone of holistic health for women, as it nurtures a deep sense of acceptance, kindness, and understanding towards oneself. By practicing self-compassion, you can cultivate greater resilience, emotional balance, and inner peace, fostering a positive relationship with yourself and enhancing your overall well-being. Recognize that self-compassion is not about self-indulgence or self-pity but rather about treating yourself with the same warmth, care, and kindness that you would offer to a dear friend or loved one.

Self-compassion enables women to navigate life's challenges with greater ease and grace, offering a powerful tool for managing stress, anxiety, and self-criticism. When faced with difficulties or setbacks, approach yourself with kindness and understanding, acknowledging your humanness and imperfections without judgment or condemnation. Practice self-compassionate self-talk by offering yourself words of encouragement, comfort, and support in moments of struggle or distress, reminding yourself that you're doing the best you can with the resources and circumstances you have.

Cultivate self-compassion by practicing mindfulness and self-awareness, tuning into your thoughts, feelings, and sensations with curiosity and non-judgmental acceptance. Notice when you're being self-critical or harsh towards yourself, and gently redirect your attention towards a more compassionate and understanding perspective. Set aside time each day for mindfulness meditation or reflection, allowing yourself to connect with your inner wisdom, intuition, and compassion, and fostering a deeper sense of self-awareness and self-acceptance.

Incorporate self-compassion into your daily self-care routine by engaging in activities that nourish your body, mind, and spirit and prioritize your well-being as a central focus of your life. Set aside time each day for self-care rituals such as journaling, reading, creative expression, or spending time in nature, and honor your needs and desires with kindness and compassion. By prioritizing self-compassion in your daily life, you can cultivate greater resilience, emotional well-being, and holistic health, empowering you to thrive in all aspects of your life as a woman.

In summary, self-compassion is essential for women's holistic health, nurturing a positive relationship with oneself and fostering greater resilience, emotional balance, and inner peace. By cultivating self-compassion through mindfulness, self-awareness, and self-care practices, you can embrace a compassionate attitude towards yourself, navigate life's challenges with greater ease and grace, and prioritize your well-being as a central focus of your life. Remember that self-compassion is a skill that can be cultivated and strengthened over time, and by approaching yourself with kindness, understanding, and acceptance, you can cultivate greater holistic health and well-being in your life.

10. Prioritize self-care and set boundaries to protect their mental and emotional well-being in today's busy world

Prioritize self-care by recognizing its importance as a non-negotiable aspect of your overall well-being. Understand that self-care is not selfish but rather a necessary investment in your physical, mental, and emotional health. Identify activities that replenish and rejuvenate you, whether it's practicing mindfulness, engaging in creative pursuits, spending time in nature, or simply relaxing with a good book. Set aside dedicated time each day for self-care activities, honoring your needs and desires as essential components of your daily routine.

Set boundaries to protect your mental and emotional well-being, recognizing that it's okay to say NO to commitments, activities, or relationships that drain your energy or compromise your well-being. Practice assertive communication by expressing your needs, preferences, and limits clearly and respectfully, and be willing to enforce boundaries when necessary to protect your time, energy, and emotional resources. Identify areas of your life where boundaries are needed, whether it's at work, in your relationships, or with technology, and take proactive steps to establish and maintain them.

Create a supportive environment that honors and respects your need for self-care and boundaries, surrounding yourself with people who uplift and empower you to prioritize your well-being. Communicate your boundaries and self-care needs with loved ones, friends, and colleagues, and enlist their support in maintaining them. Cultivate a network of support that respects and validates your boundaries, offering encouragement, understanding, and empathy as you navigate your journey towards greater balance and well-being.

Practice self-awareness and self-compassion as you navigate your self-care journey, recognizing that it's natural to encounter challenges and setbacks along the way. Be patient and gentle with yourself, acknowledging your efforts and progress, and offering yourself kindness and understanding in moments of difficulty or doubt. Set realistic goals and expectations for yourself, and celebrate your achievements and victories, no matter how small. By prioritizing self-care and setting boundaries with compassion and self-awareness, you can protect your mental and emotional well-being in today's busy world, empowering you to thrive and flourish amidst life's demands.

In summary, prioritizing self-care and setting boundaries are essential for protecting your mental and emotional well-being in today's busy world. By recognizing the importance of self-care, setting boundaries, creating a supportive environment, and practicing self-awareness and self-compassion, you can maintain balance, resilience, and vitality in your life as a woman. Remember that self-care is a journey, not a destination, and by honoring your needs and boundaries with kindness and understanding, you can cultivate greater well-being and fulfillment in all aspects of your life.

Chapter 5

Hormonal Balance and Women's Health

1. Key hormones that influence women's health, and roles they play in the body

Estrogen is a primary female sex hormone that plays a central role in reproductive health, menstrual cycle regulation, and bone density maintenance. Estrogen levels fluctuate throughout the menstrual cycle, rising during the follicular phase to stimulate ovulation and support the growth of the uterine lining, and declining during the luteal phase if fertilization does not occur. Additionally, estrogen plays a vital role in maintaining cardiovascular health, cognitive function, and mood regulation.

Progesterone is another essential female sex hormone that works in tandem with estrogen to regulate the menstrual cycle and support reproductive health. Progesterone levels rise during the luteal phase of the menstrual cycle to prepare the uterus for implantation and support early pregnancy. Additionally, progesterone helps regulate mood, promote relaxation, and support bone health, making it crucial for overall well-being.

Testosterone is often associated with male hormones but also plays a vital role in women's health, albeit in smaller quantities. Testosterone contributes to libido, energy levels, muscle mass, and bone density in women, promoting vitality and well-being. Imbalances in testosterone levels can lead to symptoms such as decreased libido, fatigue, and changes in mood and energy levels.

Thyroid hormones, including thyroxine (T4) and triiodothyronine (T3), play a crucial role in metabolism, energy production, and overall hormonal balance in women. The thyroid gland regulates the body's metabolic rate, influencing processes such as weight management, temperature regulation, and heart rate. Thyroid hormone imbalances can lead to symptoms such as fatigue, weight changes, mood disturbances, and menstrual irregularities, highlighting the importance of thyroid health for overall well-being.

In summary, estrogen, progesterone, testosterone, and thyroid hormones are key players in women's health, influencing reproductive function, mood regulation, metabolism, and overall well-being. By understanding the roles of these hormones and monitoring their balance, you can take proactive steps to support your hormonal health and optimize your overall well-being. Consider incorporating lifestyle strategies such as regular exercise, balanced nutrition, stress management, and adequate sleep to support hormonal balance and promote vitality and wellness. Additionally, consult with a healthcare provider if you experience symptoms of hormonal imbalance or have concerns about your hormonal health, as they can offer personalized guidance and support tailored to your individual needs.

2. How do hormonal fluctuations throughout the menstrual cycle impact women's physical and emotional well-being

During the follicular phase of your menstrual cycle, estrogen levels rise, leading up to ovulation. This increase in estrogen can boost energy levels, mood, and cognitive function, promoting feelings of vitality and well-being. You may notice increased motivation, creativity, and sociability during this phase, as well as enhanced physical stamina and endurance. Embrace this phase by engaging in activities that align with your energy levels, such as exercise, socializing, or pursuing creative projects.

As you approach ovulation, estrogen levels peak, triggering the release of an egg from the ovary. This surge in estrogen can heighten sensory perception, libido, and emotional sensitivity, fostering feelings of passion, connection, and intimacy. You may experience increased sexual desire, heightened sensory awareness, and enhanced emotional expression during this phase. Embrace this phase by prioritizing self-care and connection in your relationships, whether it's through intimate moments with a partner, quality time with loved ones, or self-exploration and reflection.

During the luteal phase of your menstrual cycle, progesterone levels rise, preparing the uterus for potential implantation and pregnancy. This increase in progesterone can lead to changes in mood, energy levels, and appetite, as well as physical symptoms such as bloating, breast tenderness, and fatigue. You may notice fluctuations in mood, ranging from feelings of calm and contentment to irritability or anxiety. Embrace this phase by practicing self-compassion and self-care, prioritizing rest, relaxation, and stress management techniques to support your emotional well-being.

As your menstrual cycle transitions into the menstrual phase, estrogen and progesterone levels decline, leading to the shedding of the uterine lining and the onset of menstruation. This decrease in hormones can trigger physical symptoms such as fatigue, cramps, and headaches, as well as emotional fluctuations such as sadness, irritability, or moodiness. Embrace this phase by honoring your body's needs and rhythms, allowing yourself to rest and recharge as needed, and practicing self-care rituals that promote comfort and relaxation.

In summary, hormonal fluctuations throughout the menstrual cycle can have a significant impact on your physical and emotional well-being, influencing energy levels, mood, and cognitive function. By understanding these hormonal changes and their effects on your body and mind, you can embrace each phase of your menstrual cycle with greater awareness and support. Consider tracking your menstrual cycle and symptoms to identify patterns and trends, and explore holistic strategies such as exercise, nutrition, stress management, and self-care to support your overall well-being throughout the month. Remember that your menstrual cycle is a natural and integral aspect of your health as a woman, and by honoring and nurturing your body's rhythms, you can cultivate greater vitality, resilience, and well-being.

3. What are common signs and symptoms of hormone imbalances in women, and how can they be addressed holistically?

Irregular menstrual cycles are a common sign of hormone imbalances, manifesting as missed periods, irregular bleeding, or unusually heavy or light flow. Additionally, changes in mood, such as mood swings, irritability, anxiety, or depression, can indicate hormonal fluctuations. Furthermore, physical symptoms such as fatigue, weight changes, bloating, acne, or hair loss may also point to hormone imbalances. Paying attention to these signs can provide valuable insights into your hormonal health and guide you towards holistic interventions to restore balance.

Holistic approaches to addressing hormone imbalances often focus on lifestyle modifications, including nutrition, exercise, stress management, and sleep hygiene. Prioritize nutrient-dense foods that support hormonal health, such as leafy greens, fatty fish, nuts, seeds, and whole grains. Additionally, regular exercise can help regulate hormone levels, improve mood, and promote overall well-being. Practice stress-reducing techniques such as mindfulness meditation, deep breathing exercises, or yoga to support adrenal health and reduce cortisol levels. Furthermore, prioritize restful sleep by establishing a consistent sleep schedule, creating a calming bedtime routine, and minimizing exposure to screens and stimulating activities before bedtime.

Incorporating herbal remedies and supplements into your holistic approach to hormone balance. Holy basil can help support adrenal function and promote hormone balance.

Additionally, supplements such as omega-3 fatty acids, vitamin D, magnesium, and B vitamins may support overall hormonal health and well-being. Consult with a holistic healthcare practitioner or qualified herbalist to determine the most appropriate supplements and dosages for your individual needs.

Seeking support from holistic healthcare providers such as professional health coaches, functional medicine practitioners, or integrative healthcare professionals who specialize in hormone balance and women's health. These practitioners can offer personalized guidance and treatment plans tailored to your unique hormonal profile and health goals. By taking a comprehensive and holistic approach to addressing hormone imbalances, you can restore balance and vitality to your body and mind, empowering you to thrive in all aspects of your life as a woman.

4. How can nutrition and lifestyle factors support hormonal balance in women, particularly during times of transition like puberty, pregnancy, and menopause?

During puberty (The time of life when a child experiences physical and hormonal changes that mark a transition into adulthood) your body undergoes profound changes that can influence mood, energy levels, and physical health. Nutrition plays a crucial role in supporting these changes. Focus on a balanced diet rich in whole foods, including fruits, vegetables, lean proteins, and whole grains. Incorporate foods high in essential nutrients such as calcium, iron, and omega-3 fatty acids to support bone health, energy production, and cognitive function. Additionally, staying hydrated and avoiding processed foods and excessive sugar can help maintain stable energy levels and mood. Regular physical activity, such as sports or yoga, can also support physical development and emotional well-being during this time.

During pregnancy, your nutritional needs increase to support both your health and the development of your baby. Focus on a diet rich in folate, iron, calcium, and protein to promote fetal growth and maternal health. Foods like leafy greens, legumes, lean meats, dairy products, and whole grains should be staples in your diet. Additionally, staying hydrated and consuming small, frequent meals can help manage common pregnancy symptoms such as nausea and fatigue. Incorporating gentle exercises like walking, swimming, or prenatal yoga can support physical health, reduce stress, and prepare your body for childbirth.

Menopause (The time of life when a woman's ovaries stop producing hormones and menstrual periods stop) is a significant transition that can bring about hormonal fluctuations and symptoms such as hot flashes, mood swings, and weight gain. To support hormonal balance during menopause, focus on a diet rich in phytoestrogens, found in foods like soy, flaxseeds, and whole grains, which can help alleviate some symptoms. Additionally, foods high in calcium and vitamin D, such as dairy products, fortified plant milks, and leafy greens, are essential for maintaining bone health. Regular physical activity, including strength training and cardiovascular exercises, can help manage weight, improve mood, and support overall health. Stress management techniques such as mindfulness, meditation can also reduce the impact of hormonal changes on your emotional well-being.

Across all these life stages, adopting a holistic lifestyle approach that includes adequate sleep, stress management, and avoiding harmful substances like tobacco and excessive alcohol is crucial. Ensure you get at least 7-8 hours of quality sleep each night, as sleep is vital for hormonal regulation and overall health. Incorporate stress-reducing activities into your daily routine, such as deep breathing exercises, journaling, or spending time in nature. Seek support from healthcare providers, such as nutritionists, dietitians, and holistic health practitioners, who can offer personalized guidance and support tailored to your specific needs during these transitions.

In summary, nutrition and lifestyle factors play a vital role in supporting hormonal balance during puberty, pregnancy, and menopause. By focusing on a balanced diet, regular physical activity, adequate sleep, and stress management, you can maintain your health and well-being through these significant life changes. Remember, prioritizing your needs and seeking professional support can empower you to navigate these transitions with greater ease and confidence.

5. **Holistic approaches women can explore for managing menstrual irregularities, PMS (Premenstrual syndrome) and menopausal symptoms**

To manage menstrual irregularities, it's essential to adopt a balanced diet rich in nutrients that support hormonal health. Focus on incorporating whole foods such as leafy greens, lean proteins, whole grains, and healthy fats. Foods rich in magnesium, like nuts, seeds, and dark chocolate, can help regulate menstrual cycles and reduce cramps. Practicing yoga and mindfulness meditation can also help reduce stress, which is a common factor in menstrual irregularities. Create a food journal to track your intake and notice patterns or improvements.

PMS can be managed effectively through lifestyle adjustments and natural remedies. Regular exercise, such as walking, swimming, or yoga, can alleviate symptoms by boosting endorphin levels and improving mood. Dietary changes, such as reducing caffeine, sugar, and salt intake, can help minimize bloating and irritability. Incorporating foods high in vitamin B6, calcium, and magnesium can alleviate PMS symptoms. Additionally, using essential oils like lavender or chamomile for aromatherapy can reduce anxiety and promote relaxation. Develop a daily self-care routine that includes physical activity, balanced nutrition, and relaxation techniques to mitigate PMS symptoms.

Menopausal symptoms like hot flashes, night sweats, and mood swings can be addressed with holistic approaches. Staying active with weight-bearing exercises can help maintain bone density and overall health. Practicing mindfulness and stress-reducing activities can improve emotional well-being and reduce the severity of menopausal symptoms. Keeping a symptom diary can help you identify triggers and effective remedies, allowing you to tailor your approach to your specific needs.

Hydration and sleep are critical components of managing menstrual irregularities, PMS, and menopausal symptoms. Ensure you drink plenty of water throughout the day to stay hydrated, which can reduce bloating and improve overall health. Prioritize quality sleep by creating a calming bedtime routine, avoiding screens before bed, and ensuring your sleep environment is comfortable and cool. Supplements like melatonin or magnesium can support better sleep quality. Schedule regular wellness check-ups with a healthcare provider to monitor your hormonal health and make informed decisions about your holistic approach.

In summary, managing menstrual irregularities, PMS, and menopausal symptoms can be achieved through a combination of balanced nutrition, regular exercise, and stress-reduction techniques. By adopting these holistic approaches and staying attuned to your body's needs, you can alleviate symptoms and enhance your overall well-being. Remember to track your progress, consult with healthcare professionals when needed, and make adjustments to your routine to find what works best for you.

6. How do stress, sleep, and environmental factors affect women's hormone levels, and what strategies can women use to mitigate these effects?

Chronic stress can significantly impact your hormone levels by elevating cortisol, the body's primary stress hormone. High cortisol levels can disrupt the balance of other hormones, such as estrogen and progesterone, leading to irregular menstrual cycles, mood swings, and fatigue. To manage stress effectively, consider incorporating relaxation techniques such as deep breathing exercises, mindfulness meditation, or yoga into your daily routine. Set aside time each day for activities that bring you joy and relaxation, whether it's reading, gardening, or spending time with loved ones. By prioritizing self-care and stress management, you can reduce cortisol levels and support hormonal balance.

Adequate sleep is crucial for maintaining hormonal health. Poor sleep can disrupt the production of essential hormones like melatonin, which regulates sleep-wake cycles, and growth hormone, which plays a role in tissue repair and metabolism. Additionally, lack of sleep can lead to increased cortisol levels, further exacerbating hormonal imbalances. To improve sleep quality, establish a consistent sleep schedule by going to bed and waking up at the same time each day. Create a calming bedtime routine, such as taking a warm bath, practicing gentle stretches, or listening to soothing music. Ensure your sleep environment is conducive to rest by keeping it cool, dark, and quiet. If you struggle with sleep issues, consider limiting caffeine and screen time before bed to promote better sleep hygiene.

Environmental factors, such as exposure to endocrine-disrupting chemicals (EDCs), can negatively impact hormone levels. EDCs are found in everyday items like plastics, personal care products, and household cleaners, and can mimic or interfere with the body's natural hormones. To reduce exposure to EDCs, opt for natural and organic personal care products, and avoid plastics that contain BPA (chemical used in plastic) by choosing glass or stainless steel containers for food and beverages. Additionally, use eco-friendly cleaning products free from harmful chemicals. Regularly ventilate your living spaces and consider investing in air purifiers to reduce indoor pollutants. By making mindful choices about the products you use, you can minimize exposure to EDCs and support your hormonal health.

Holistic strategies such as balanced nutrition, regular physical activity, and mindful living can further support hormonal balance. Focus on a nutrient-dense diet rich in whole foods, such as fruits, vegetables, lean proteins, and healthy fats, to provide your body with the essential nutrients it needs for optimal hormonal function. Incorporate regular exercise, such as walking, swimming, or yoga, to boost mood, reduce stress, and improve overall health. Practice mindfulness techniques, such as meditation or journaling, to enhance emotional resilience and maintain a positive outlook. By adopting these holistic lifestyle changes, you can create a supportive environment for your hormones and overall well-being.

In summary, stress, sleep, and environmental factors significantly affect hormone levels, but you can mitigate these effects through mindful lifestyle choices. Prioritize stress management, ensure adequate sleep, reduce exposure to harmful chemicals, and embrace holistic strategies to support your hormonal health. By taking proactive steps to care for your body and mind, you can achieve greater balance and vitality in your everyday life.

7. How can women advocate for themselves in healthcare settings to receive personalized support for hormonal health?

Advocating for yourself in healthcare settings to receive personalized support for hormonal health is crucial. It ensures that your unique needs are recognized and addressed. Let's explore how you can effectively advocate for yourself, empowering you to take charge of your hormonal health.

Education is your most powerful tool. Understanding your body and the intricacies of hormonal health will give you the confidence to speak up and ask the right questions. Research common hormonal issues, symptoms, and treatments so you are well-informed about what you might be experiencing. Keep a detailed journal of your symptoms, noting when they occur, their severity, and any patterns you observe. This journal will serve as a valuable resource when discussing your concerns with healthcare providers, helping them understand your situation better. Make a list of questions and concerns to discuss during your appointments, ensuring you cover all aspects of your health.

Choose a healthcare provider who listens to you and respects your concerns. It's essential to find a doctor or health coach who takes your symptoms seriously and works with you to find the best solutions. Don't hesitate to seek a second opinion if you feel your concerns are not being adequately addressed. During appointments, be clear and concise about your symptoms and how they affect your daily life. Assertively communicate your needs and preferences, and don't be afraid to ask for explanations or clarifications about any proposed treatments or tests. Remember, a good healthcare provider will welcome your questions and work with you to develop a personalized care plan.

Familiarize yourself with available diagnostic tests and treatment options. Understanding the various methods used to assess hormonal health, such as blood tests, saliva tests, and ultrasounds, can help you advocate for comprehensive evaluations. If you believe a specific test is necessary based on your symptoms and research, request it. Similarly, be aware of both conventional and alternative treatment options, including lifestyle changes, supplements, and medications. Discuss these options with your healthcare provider, weighing the benefits and risks of each. Collaborate on a treatment plan that aligns with your health goals and personal preferences.

Build a support network. Connect with other women who have similar experiences through support groups, online forums, or local community groups. Sharing your journey with others can provide emotional support and practical advice. Additionally, consider involving a trusted friend or family member in your healthcare appointments for added support and to help you remember important details. Advocate for yourself outside of medical settings as well by promoting workplace policies that support women's health, such as flexible work hours and accommodations for medical appointments.

In summary, advocating for yourself in healthcare settings involves educating yourself about hormonal health, choosing a supportive healthcare provider, understanding diagnostic and treatment options, and building a support network. By taking these proactive steps, you can ensure that your hormonal health is managed in a personalized and effective manner. Remember, you are your own best advocate, and your health and well-being are worth fighting for.

8. How can women tune into their bodies' signals and intuition to better understand and support their hormonal health?

Tuning into your body's signals and intuition is a powerful way to understand and support your hormonal health. By paying close attention to how you feel physically and emotionally, you can identify patterns and make informed decisions that promote balance and well-being.

Start by practicing mindfulness and self-awareness. Take time each day to check in with yourself, observing any physical sensations, emotions, or changes in your body. Keeping a journal can be incredibly helpful. Record details about your menstrual cycle, including the start and end dates, the flow's heaviness, and any symptoms like cramps, headaches, or mood swings. Note your energy levels, sleep quality, and any stressors or significant events. Over time, you'll begin to see patterns that can provide valuable insights into your hormonal health.

Listen to your intuition when it comes to your health and well-being. Your body often sends subtle signals when something is off balance. If you feel unusually fatigued, experience persistent mood changes, or notice irregularities in your menstrual cycle, trust that your body is trying to communicate with you. Don't ignore these signs. Instead, seek to understand them by consulting with a healthcare provider who respects your insights and is willing to work with you to uncover the root cause. Remember, you know your body better than anyone else.

To support this process, develop a daily self-care routine that includes practices aimed at promoting hormonal balance. Incorporate activities like gentle yoga, meditation, or deep breathing exercises to reduce stress and enhance mind-body connection. Ensure you get adequate sleep, eat a balanced diet rich in whole foods, and stay hydrated. Regular physical activity, such as walking or swimming, can also help regulate hormones. By prioritizing these self-care practices, you'll create an environment that supports hormonal health and allows you to better tune into your body's needs.

Establish an action plan to maintain and improve your hormonal health. Set specific, achievable goals based on the patterns and signals you've observed. For example, if you notice that stress significantly impacts your menstrual cycle, prioritize stress-reduction techniques and perhaps seek support from a therapist or counselor. If you find that certain foods affect your energy levels or mood, adjust your diet accordingly. Regularly review and adjust your self-care routine and goals as needed, always keeping your well-being at the forefront.

In summary, tuning into your body's signals and intuition is essential for understanding and supporting your hormonal health. By practicing mindfulness, trusting your instincts, developing a supportive self-care routine, and creating a personalized action plan, you can take proactive steps toward achieving greater balance and vitality. Remember, your body is your most reliable guide, and by listening to it, you can empower yourself to make informed and healthful choices.

Chapter 6

Self-Care Rituals for Women

1. What is self-care, and why is it essential for women's holistic well-being?

Self-care is the practice of taking deliberate actions to maintain and improve your physical, mental, and emotional health. It involves prioritizing your own needs and well-being, allowing you to better manage stress, prevent burnout, and lead a balanced and fulfilling life. For women, self-care is particularly essential as it addresses the unique challenges and pressures you may face, ensuring you have the resilience and strength to thrive in all areas of your life.

Self-care is about recognizing that your well-being is a priority, not a luxury. In our fast-paced world, women often juggle multiple roles and responsibilities, from careers and family to social obligations and personal goals. This constant balancing act can lead to stress, fatigue, and neglect of your own needs. By incorporating self-care into your daily routine, you create a foundation of health and happiness that supports every aspect of your life. It's not about being selfish; it's about understanding that you cannot pour from an empty cup.

To make self-care a regular part of your life, start by identifying activities that rejuvenate and energize you. This could include physical activities like yoga, dancing, or hiking, which boost your physical health and release endorphins. Mental self-care might involve reading a book, journaling, or engaging in hobbies that stimulate your creativity. Emotional self-care can include spending time with loved ones, practicing gratitude, or seeking therapy or counseling when needed. Create a self-care plan that incorporates these activities into your daily and weekly routines, ensuring you dedicate time to nurture yourself regularly.

Setting boundaries is a critical component of self-care. Learning to say no to demands that overwhelm you or compromise your well-being is vital. This might mean setting limits on work hours, declining social invitations when you need rest, or delegating household tasks to others. Communicate your boundaries clearly and kindly to those around you, explaining the importance of self-care in maintaining your overall health. By doing so, you create a supportive environment where your needs are respected and met.

In summary, self-care is essential for women's holistic well-being because it ensures you are physically, mentally, and emotionally nourished. By making self-care a priority, identifying rejuvenating activities, setting clear boundaries, and creating a personalized self-care plan, you can enhance your quality of life and achieve a greater sense of balance and fulfillment. Remember, taking care of yourself is the first step to being able to care for others and meet the demands of daily life with energy and joy.

2   How can women identify their individual self-care needs and preferences?

Identifying your individual self-care needs and preferences is a personal journey that requires introspection and experimentation. It's about understanding what uniquely nourishes you and supports your overall well-being. Let's explore how you can discover and embrace your self-care needs, making them a fundamental part of your daily life.

Start by assessing your current state of well-being. Take a moment to reflect on various aspects of your life—physical health, mental clarity, emotional stability, and social connections. Notice any areas where you feel depleted, stressed, or unfulfilled. Ask yourself questions like, "When do I feel my best?" and "What activities leave me feeling refreshed and energized?" Writing down your thoughts in a journal can help clarify your needs and reveal patterns that may not be immediately obvious.

Experiment with different self-care activities to discover what resonates with you. There's no one-size-fits-all approach to self-care; it's about finding what works best for you. Try incorporating a variety of activities into your routine, such as physical exercise, meditation, creative pursuits, and social interactions. Pay attention to how each activity makes you feel and adjust accordingly. For example, you might find that a morning yoga session sets a positive tone for your day, or that reading before bed helps you unwind and sleep better. Keep a record of your experiences and note which activities provide the most benefit.

Creating a self-care action plan tailored to your preferences is the next step. Based on your reflections and experiments, identify the activities that bring you the most joy and relaxation. Schedule these activities into your daily or weekly routine, treating them as non-negotiable appointments with yourself. If you enjoy nature walks, set aside time each week to explore a local park. If journaling helps you process emotions, make it a daily habit. By prioritizing these activities, you ensure that self-care becomes an integral part of your life, rather than an afterthought.

Regularly reassess your self-care needs and adjust your plan as necessary. Your needs may change over time due to life circumstances, stress levels, or personal growth. Periodically take stock of how you're feeling and whether your self-care activities are still effective. Be flexible and willing to try new things if your current routine isn't meeting your needs. It's also helpful to seek feedback from trusted friends or a therapist who can offer insights and support as you refine your self-care practice.

In summary, identifying your individual self-care needs and preferences involves self-reflection, experimentation, and intentional planning. By assessing your well-being, trying different activities, creating a personalized action plan, and regularly reassessing your needs, you can build a self-care routine that truly supports your holistic health. Remember, taking the time to care for yourself is a vital investment in your overall well-being and happiness.

3 Some examples of self-care rituals that women can incorporate into their daily, weekly, and monthly routines

Incorporating self-care rituals into your daily, weekly, and monthly routines is a powerful way to nurture your well-being and maintain balance in your life. These rituals can vary widely depending on your personal preferences and needs, but the key is consistency and intentionality. Let's explore some examples and actionable steps you can take to integrate them into your life.

These are small, manageable activities that can fit seamlessly into your everyday routine. Start your day with a few minutes of mindfulness meditation or deep breathing exercises to set a calm and focused tone. Incorporate physical activity, whether it's a morning yoga session, a brisk walk, or a quick workout. Make time for nourishing meals and stay hydrated throughout the day. In the evening, establish a wind-down routine that might include reading, journaling, or a warm bath to help you relax and prepare for restful sleep. Create a daily action plan that outlines these activities and sets aside specific times for each, ensuring they become habitual.

Weekly self-care rituals can be more involved and serve as opportunities to reset and recharge. Dedicate time for activities that bring you joy and relaxation. This could include a longer exercise session, such as a hike or a dance class, or engaging in creative pursuits like painting or cooking a new recipe. Schedule social time with friends or family, whether it's a coffee date, a movie night, or a virtual hangout. Consider setting aside an hour or two for self-reflection and goal-setting, reviewing the past week and planning for the week ahead. Use a planner or calendar to block out these times, treating them as important appointments that you commit to keeping.

Monthly self-care rituals can focus on deeper reflection and self-improvement. Plan a personal retreat day where you disconnect from your usual responsibilities and spend time doing things that nourish your soul. This could involve a spa day, a solo hike, or simply a day at home filled with activities you love. Review your progress on personal goals and set new intentions for the coming month. Consider booking a session with a therapist or life coach to explore any challenges and gain new perspectives. Incorporate these monthly rituals into your calendar, ensuring you have dedicated time for deeper self-care and reflection.

To ensure these rituals become a consistent part of your life, create a self-care action plan. Start by listing the daily, weekly, and monthly activities that resonate most with you. Next, block out specific times in your schedule for each activity, treating them as non-negotiable commitments. Set reminders on your phone or use a planner to help you stay on track. Regularly review and adjust your plan as needed, ensuring it continues to meet your evolving needs. By making self-care a priority and embedding these rituals into your routine, you'll cultivate a more balanced, joyful, and fulfilling life.

In summary, incorporating self-care rituals into your daily, weekly, and monthly routines can significantly enhance your overall well-being. By identifying activities that nourish you and creating a structured action plan, you ensure that self-care becomes a regular, integral part of your life. Remember, consistent self-care is essential for maintaining balance, reducing stress, and promoting long-term health and happiness.

4 How do self-care practices like skincare, massage, and relaxation techniques nourish the body, mind, and spirit?

Self-care practices such as skincare, massage, and relaxation techniques offer multifaceted benefits that nourish the body, mind, and spirit, promoting holistic well-being. Let's delve into how these practices contribute to your overall health and provide actionable steps to incorporate them into your life.

Skincare rituals go beyond superficial beauty; they provide an opportunity to connect with your body and cultivate self-love. Through gentle cleansing, moisturizing, and pampering your skin, you not only enhance its health and appearance but also foster a sense of nurturing and self-appreciation. Consider establishing a daily skincare routine that includes cleansing, toning, moisturizing, and applying sunscreen to protect your skin from environmental damage. Set aside a few minutes each morning and evening to care for your skin, treating it as a sacred self-care ritual that honors your body.

Massage is another powerful self-care practice that offers both physical and emotional benefits. Beyond its ability to relieve muscle tension and promote relaxation, massage can stimulate the release of endorphins, the body's natural feel-good hormones, leading to a sense of bliss and well-being. Treat yourself to a professional massage or incorporate self-massage techniques into your routine using a foam roller, massage ball, or your hands. Focus on areas of tension or discomfort, applying gentle pressure and mindful touch to release tight muscles and promote circulation. Regular massage sessions can become a cherished part of your self-care regimen, providing both physical relief and emotional nourishment.

Relaxation techniques, such as deep breathing, meditation, and guided imagery, offer profound benefits for the mind, body, and spirit. By practicing these techniques regularly, you can reduce stress levels, calm the nervous system, and cultivate a sense of inner peace and balance. Incorporate relaxation into your daily routine by carving out time for mindfulness meditation or deep breathing exercises. Find a quiet, comfortable space where you can sit or lie down without distractions. Close your eyes, take slow, deep breaths, and focus your attention on the present moment. Visualize a peaceful scene or repeat a calming mantra to quiet the chatter of the mind. Aim to practice relaxation techniques for at least 10-15 minutes each day, gradually increasing the duration as you become more comfortable.

In summary, self-care practices like skincare, massage, and relaxation techniques offer holistic nourishment for the body, mind, and spirit. By incorporating these practices into your daily routine and treating them as sacred rituals, you can enhance your overall well-being and cultivate a deeper connection with yourself. Remember, self-care is not selfish; it's an essential investment in your health and happiness. Commit to prioritizing your well-being through these nurturing practices, and watch as they transform your life from the inside out.

5   How can women prioritize self-care without feeling guilty or selfish?

Prioritizing self-care can feel challenging for many women, as societal expectations and cultural norms often prioritize the needs of others over our own. However, it's essential to recognize that self-care isn't selfish; it's a necessary investment in your well-being that enables you to show up fully for yourself and others. To overcome feelings of guilt or selfishness, it's crucial to reframe your mindset and develop healthy habits that prioritize self-care.

Start by acknowledging that self-care is a fundamental aspect of maintaining balance and resilience in your life. Just as you wouldn't expect a car to run without regular maintenance, you can't expect yourself to function optimally without taking care of your physical, mental, and emotional needs. Recognize that prioritizing self-care isn't a luxury or indulgence but a vital component of overall health and happiness.

Challenge any limiting beliefs or internalized narratives that contribute to feelings of guilt or selfishness. Remind yourself that you are deserving of love, care, and attention, just like anyone else. Consider the analogy of putting on your oxygen mask first before assisting others on an airplane; by taking care of yourself, you're better equipped to support those around you. Reframe self-care as an act of self-respect and empowerment rather than self-indulgence.

Develop a personalized self-care action plan that aligns with your needs, preferences, and values. Identify activities and practices that replenish your energy, reduce stress, and bring you joy. This might include carving out time for exercise, meditation, hobbies, or spending quality time with loved ones. Schedule these activities into your daily or weekly routine and treat them as non-negotiable appointments with yourself. By proactively prioritizing self-care, you're sending a clear message to yourself and others that your well-being matters.

Practice self-compassion and give yourself permission to prioritize self-care without guilt. Recognize that you're doing the best you can with the resources and circumstances you have. Be gentle with yourself on days when self-care feels challenging or doesn't go as planned. Remember that self-care isn't about perfection but about making conscious choices to honor your needs and nurture your well-being. By cultivating a mindset of self-compassion and resilience, you can navigate feelings of guilt or selfishness with greater ease and prioritize self-care as an essential aspect of your daily life.

6 What role do boundaries play in self-care, and how can women assertively communicate their needs and limits?

Boundaries are essential for self-care as they define the limits of what is acceptable and respectful in our interactions with others. They serve as a protective barrier, safeguarding our physical, emotional, and mental well-being. Women often struggle with setting boundaries due to societal expectations to be accommodating and nurturing. However, asserting boundaries is crucial for maintaining a healthy balance and preventing burnout.

To assertively communicate your needs and limits, start by understanding your boundaries and what feels comfortable and respectful to you. Reflect on situations where you feel overextended or drained, and identify the behaviors or circumstances that violate your boundaries. This could include saying no to excessive demands, setting aside time for yourself, or speaking up when someone crosses a boundary. Clarify your boundaries internally before communicating them to others.

Once you're clear about your boundaries, practice assertive communication when expressing them to others. Use "I" statements to assert your needs without blaming or accusing others. For example, instead of saying, "You always expect too much from me," you could say, "I feel overwhelmed when I have too many tasks to handle. Can we discuss how to better distribute responsibilities?" Be firm and direct while maintaining a respectful tone.

Set specific boundaries and consequences for when they're crossed. Clearly communicate your limits and the consequences for violating them. For example, if a colleague consistently interrupts your personal time with work-related requests, you could say, "I'm unavailable after 7 p.m. for work-related matters. If it's urgent, please email me, and I'll address it first thing in the morning." Follow through with the consequences if necessary to reinforce the importance of respecting your boundaries.

Practice self-compassion and assertiveness as you navigate setting and enforcing boundaries. Recognize that it's natural to feel uncomfortable or guilty when asserting boundaries, especially if you're accustomed to prioritizing others' needs over your own. Remind yourself that boundaries are essential for your well-being and that asserting them is an act of self-care, not selfishness. Give yourself permission to prioritize your needs and advocate for yourself with kindness and firmness.

In summary, boundaries play a vital role in self-care by protecting our well-being and preserving our autonomy and dignity. By understanding our boundaries, practicing assertive communication, setting clear boundaries and consequences, and cultivating self-compassion, women can assertively communicate their needs and limits, fostering healthier relationships and greater well-being. Remember that setting boundaries is not only a form of self-respect but also a necessary step toward creating a balanced and fulfilling life.

7 How can women create a calming and supportive self-care environment at home?

Creating a calming and supportive self-care environment at home is essential for nurturing your well-being and promoting relaxation and rejuvenation. Here are some steps you can take to cultivate a tranquil and supportive space that encourages self-care:

Declutter and organize your living space to create a sense of order and tranquility. Remove any unnecessary items and streamline your belongings to reduce visual clutter and promote a sense of calm. Consider incorporating elements of nature, such as plants or natural materials, to bring the outdoors inside and create a soothing atmosphere.

Arrange your furniture and decor in a way that promotes flow and openness, allowing energy to move freely throughout the space.

Personalize your environment with items that bring you comfort and joy. Surround yourself with meaningful objects, such as photographs, artwork, or sentimental items that evoke positive emotions and memories. Choose colors and textures that resonate with you and promote relaxation, such as soft neutrals, warm earth tones, or calming blues and greens. Incorporate cozy blankets, pillows, and soft lighting to create a cozy and inviting ambiance.

Establish designated areas for self-care activities that support your physical, mental, and emotional well-being. Dedicate a corner of your home to mindfulness practices like meditation or yoga, complete with a comfortable cushion or mat and any props or accessories you may need. Create a cozy reading corner with a comfortable chair or sofa and a selection of books or magazines that inspire and uplift you. Set up a calming bath area with candles, essential oils, and luxurious bath products for indulgent self-care rituals.

Prioritize calmness and relaxation by minimizing noise and distractions in your home environment. Consider implementing soundproofing measures, such as heavy curtains or rugs, to dampen noise from outside sources. Create a peaceful ambiance with soothing soundscape, such as nature sounds, gentle music, or white noise, to mask any disruptive noises and promote relaxation. Establish boundaries with family members or roommates to ensure that you have dedicated time and space for self-care without interruptions.

In summary, creating a calming and supportive self-care environment at home involves decluttering and organizing your space, personalizing your environment with meaningful items, establishing designated areas for self-care activities, and minimizing noise and distractions. By intentionally designing your living space to promote tranquility and relaxation, you can enhance your overall well-being and cultivate a sanctuary where you can retreat and recharge whenever needed. Remember that your home is a reflection of your inner state, so investing time and effort into creating a nurturing environment can have profound effects on your physical, mental, and emotional health.

8 Some self-care activities that women can engage in during times of stress or overwhelm

During times of stress or overwhelm, engaging in self-care activities is crucial for restoring balance and promoting well-being. Here are some self-care activities that women can incorporate into their routine to manage stress and overwhelm effectively:

Prioritize activities that promote relaxation and mindfulness, such as deep breathing exercises, meditation, or progressive muscle relaxation. These practices help calm the nervous system, reduce tension, and cultivate a sense of inner peace and clarity. Dedicate a few minutes each day to practice deep breathing or mindfulness meditation, focusing on the present moment and letting go of worries and distractions. Set aside a quiet space where you can practice these activities without interruptions, and consider using guided meditation apps or online resources to enhance your experience.

Physical activity is another powerful self-care tool for managing stress and overwhelm. Engage in activities that get your body moving and release endorphins, such as yoga, walking, dancing, or jogging. Choose activities that you enjoy and that align with your fitness level and preferences. Incorporate movement into your daily routine by taking short breaks throughout the day to stretch or go for a brisk walk. Schedule regular exercise sessions into your calendar to ensure consistency and prioritize your physical well-being.

Creative expression can be a therapeutic outlet for processing emotions and reducing stress. Engage in activities that allow you to express yourself creatively, such as painting, writing, crafting, or playing music. Set aside time each day to engage in a creative pursuit that brings you joy and helps you unwind. Create a dedicated space in your home where you can explore your creativity freely, whether it's a cozy corner with art supplies or a writing desk with inspiring decor. Allow yourself to experiment and play without judgment, focusing on the process rather than the outcome.

Prioritize self-care activities that nourish your body and promote overall well-being. This could include indulging in a warm bath with essential oils and Epsom salts, treating yourself to a spa day at home with skincare treatments and pampering rituals, or enjoying a healthy and nourishing meal that fuels your body and mind. Practice self-compassion and give yourself permission to prioritize your needs, even when life feels hectic and overwhelming. Remember that self-care isn't selfish; it's a necessary investment in your health and happiness.

In summary, during times of stress or overwhelm, engaging in self-care activities is essential for managing your well-being and restoring balance. Prioritize relaxation and mindfulness practices, incorporate physical activity into your routine, express yourself creatively, and nourish your body with healthy habits. By making self-care a priority and incorporating these activities into your daily life, you can effectively manage stress and overwhelm and cultivate a greater sense of resilience and well-being.

9 How can women practice self-compassion and kindness as part of their self-care routines?

Practicing self-compassion and kindness is a vital aspect of self-care that allows women to cultivate a nurturing and supportive relationship with themselves. Here are some strategies to incorporate self-compassion and kindness into your self-care routine:

Cultivate self-awareness and mindfulness to recognize when you're being self-critical or judgmental. Pay attention to your inner dialogue and notice any negative thoughts or self-limiting beliefs that arise. Instead of engaging with these thoughts, practice self-compassion by offering yourself kindness and understanding. Treat yourself as you would a dear friend, offering words of encouragement and reassurance in moments of difficulty or self-doubt.

Practice self-care activities that nourish your body, mind, and spirit and prioritize your well-being. This could include engaging in activities that bring you joy and relaxation, such as taking a leisurely walk in nature, practicing yoga or meditation, enjoying a soothing bath, or indulging in your favorite hobbies. Set aside dedicated time each day for self-care rituals that replenish your energy and promote self-compassion and kindness towards yourself.

Challenge perfectionism and unrealistic expectations by embracing imperfection and self-acceptance. Recognize that it's okay to make mistakes and experience setbacks; it's a natural part of being human. Instead of striving for perfection, focus on progress and growth, celebrating your achievements and efforts along the way. Practice self-compassion by treating yourself with patience, gentleness, and understanding, especially during challenging times or when facing obstacles.

Surround yourself with supportive and nurturing relationships that uplift and empower you. Seek out friends, family members, or mentors who offer compassion, encouragement, and validation. Share your struggles and vulnerabilities with trusted loved ones, knowing that you're not alone in your experiences. Create a network of support that celebrates your strengths and helps you navigate life's ups and downs with resilience and grace.

In summary, practicing self-compassion and kindness as part of your self-care routine is essential for nurturing your well-being and cultivating a positive relationship with yourself. By cultivating self-awareness, engaging in nurturing self-care activities, challenging perfectionism, and surrounding yourself with supportive relationships, you can foster a greater sense of self-compassion and kindness in your life. Remember that you deserve love, kindness, and compassion, and treating yourself with the same care and understanding that you offer others is a powerful form of self-care.

10 How can self-care rituals deepen women's connection to themselves and foster a sense of empowerment and resilience?

Self-care rituals have the power to deepen women's connection to themselves and foster a profound sense of empowerment and resilience. Here's how incorporating self-care rituals into your routine can cultivate these positive qualities:

Self-care rituals provide an opportunity for introspection and self-reflection, allowing women to tune into their inner needs and desires. By taking the time to prioritize self-care activities that nourish the body, mind, and spirit, you create a sacred space for self-discovery and self-awareness. Engaging in rituals such as meditation, journaling, or mindfulness practices enables you to cultivate a deeper understanding of yourself, your values, and your goals, fostering a stronger connection to your inner wisdom and intuition.

Self-care rituals promote a sense of empowerment by putting you in the driver's seat of your own well-being. When you actively engage in activities that support your physical, mental, and emotional health, you take ownership of your life and prioritize your needs and priorities. By making self-care a non-negotiable part of your routine, you send a powerful message to yourself and others that your well-being matters and that you are worthy of love, care, and attention. This sense of agency and empowerment boosts your confidence and self-esteem, empowering you to navigate life's challenges with resilience and grace.

Self-care rituals cultivate resilience by providing a source of strength and support during times of adversity. By building a foundation of self-care practices that nourish and sustain you, you develop the inner resources needed to cope with stress, overcome obstacles, and bounce back from setbacks. Engaging in rituals that promote relaxation, mindfulness, and self-compassion helps you recharge your batteries and replenish your energy reserves, enabling you to face life's challenges with a greater sense of clarity, calm, and resilience.

Self-care rituals foster a deeper connection to your intuition and inner guidance, empowering you to make decisions that align with your values and priorities. When you take the time to nurture yourself and honor your needs, you create space for your intuition to speak and guide you towards paths that are in alignment with your highest good. Trusting in your intuition and inner wisdom strengthens your sense of self-trust and self-reliance, empowering you to make choices that honor your authenticity and lead to greater fulfillment and joy.

In summary, self-care rituals deepen women's connection to themselves and foster a sense of empowerment and resilience by promoting self-awareness, agency, strength, and intuition. By incorporating self-care practices into your daily routine and prioritizing activities that nourish and sustain you, you cultivate a profound sense of self-love, self-worth, and self-trust, empowering you to navigate life's ups and downs with grace and confidence. Remember that self-care isn't selfish; it's an essential investment in your well-being and an act of self-love that fuels your growth and empowers you to shine your brightest light in the world.

Chapter 7

Spirituality and Inner Growth

1. What is spirituality, and how does it differ from religion

Spirituality is a deeply personal and introspective journey characterized by a profound sense of connection to something greater than oneself. It involves exploring questions of meaning, purpose, and existence, and seeking a deeper understanding of one's inner self and the world around them. Unlike religion, which often involves adherence to specific doctrines, rituals, and organized institutions, spirituality is more flexible and individualized, allowing individuals to explore their beliefs and practices in a way that resonates with their unique experiences and perspectives.

For those seeking to delve into their spirituality, there are several action plans that can be undertaken. Firstly, take time for self-reflection and introspection to gain insight into your beliefs, values, and experiences. This can be achieved through journaling, meditation, or engaging in meaningful conversations with trusted individuals. Secondly, seek out opportunities for spiritual exploration and growth, such as attending workshops, retreats, or joining community groups focused on spirituality. These experiences can offer valuable insights and support along your journey.

Thirdly, incorporate spiritual practices into your daily life to nurture your connection to yourself and the world around you. This could involve practices like mindfulness meditation, spending time in nature, or engaging in acts of kindness and compassion. By making these practices a regular part of your routine, you can deepen your spiritual connection and cultivate a greater sense of inner peace and fulfillment. Lastly, stay open to new experiences and perspectives, allowing yourself to evolve and grow along your spiritual journey. Be curious, adventurous, and willing to explore different paths and practices that resonate with your heart and soul. Remember that spirituality is a deeply personal journey, and there's no one-size-fits-all approach. Trust your intuition and follow the path that feels most authentic and meaningful to you.

In summary, spirituality is an individualized journey focused on seeking connection to something greater than oneself, exploring questions of meaning and purpose, and deepening understanding of the inner self and the world. Unlike religion, which often involves adherence to specific doctrines and rituals, spirituality offers flexibility and personalization, allowing individuals to explore beliefs and practices according to their unique experiences and perspectives. To embark on a spiritual journey, individuals can engage in self-reflection, seek out opportunities for growth and exploration, incorporate spiritual practices into daily life, and remain open to new experiences and perspectives along the way. Through these actions, individuals can nurture their spiritual connection, cultivate inner peace and fulfillment, and evolve on their journey of self-discovery and growth.

2. **How can women cultivate a sense of spirituality and connection to something greater than themselves?**

Cultivating a sense of spirituality and connection to something greater than oneself is a deeply personal journey that can bring profound meaning and fulfillment to a woman's life. Here are some steps you can take to embark on this journey:

Carve out time for self-reflection and introspection. Set aside moments in your day for quiet contemplation, journaling, or meditation to explore your inner thoughts, beliefs, and values. Reflect on experiences that have shaped your understanding of the world and contemplate the deeper questions of existence and purpose. By delving into your innermost thoughts and feelings, you can begin to cultivate a deeper sense of self-awareness and connection to your inner spirit.

Seek out opportunities for spiritual exploration and growth. Attend workshops, retreats, or classes focused on spirituality that resonate with your interests and values. Engage in conversations with like-minded individuals who share your curiosity and openness to exploring the mysteries of life. Surround yourself with supportive communities that encourage growth and provide a safe space for asking questions and sharing insights. By immersing yourself in environments that nourish your spiritual curiosity, you can expand your perspective and deepen your connection to something greater than yourself.

Incorporate spiritual practices into your daily routine. Experiment with mindfulness meditation, prayer, or breathing technique to center yourself and cultivate a sense of presence and inner peace. Spend time in nature, whether it's taking a leisurely walk in the park, gardening, or stargazing, to connect with the beauty and wonder of the natural world. Engage in acts of kindness and compassion, such as volunteering or offering support to those in need, to cultivate a sense of interconnectedness and service to others. By integrating these practices into your daily life, you can foster a deeper sense of spirituality and connection to the divine.

Stay open to the signs and synchronicities that may guide you along your spiritual journey. Pay attention to moments of serendipity, intuition, and inspiration that arise in your life. Trust your inner guidance and allow yourself to be led by your intuition toward experiences and opportunities that resonate with your soul's deepest longings. By embracing curiosity, openness, and trust in the unfolding of your spiritual path, you can cultivate a sense of spirituality and connection that enriches every aspect of your life.

3. Some spiritual practices that women can explore.

Exploring spiritual practices can be a deeply enriching journey that nurtures your connection to yourself and the world around you. Here are some practices you can explore to deepen your spirituality:

Meditation is a powerful practice that can help quiet the mind, reduce stress, and cultivate inner peace. Set aside time each day to sit in quiet contemplation, focusing on your breath or a mantra to center yourself and connect with your inner being. Start with just a few minutes each day and gradually increase the duration as you become more comfortable with the practice. Experiment with different meditation techniques, such as mindfulness meditation, loving-kindness meditation, or guided visualization, to find what resonates most with you.

Prayer is a deeply personal and sacred practice that can foster a sense of connection to the divine. Whether you follow a specific religious tradition or prefer a more eclectic approach, prayer can be a way to express gratitude, seek guidance, or offer blessings to yourself and others. Set aside time each day to pray, either silently or aloud, expressing your hopes, fears, and intentions with sincerity and reverence. Create a sacred space in your home where you can pray, surrounded by meaningful symbols, candles, or sacred objects that inspire and uplift you.

Connecting with nature is a profound way to nurture your spiritual connection and cultivate a sense of wonder and reverence for the natural world. Spend time outdoors, whether it's taking a walk in the woods, sitting by a lake, or watching the sunrise or sunset, and allow yourself to be fully present in the moment. Notice the sights, sounds, and sensations of nature around you, and allow yourself to feel a sense of interconnectedness with all of creation. Practice gratitude for the beauty and abundance of the earth, and commit to being a steward of the planet, caring for and protecting the natural world for future generations.

Exploring creative expression can be a powerful way to tap into your spirituality and connect with your innermost thoughts and feelings. Engage in activities such as journaling, painting, dancing, or playing music as a way to express yourself and explore your spiritual journey. Set aside time each day to engage in a creative pursuit that brings you joy and allows you to express your deepest emotions and insights. Allow yourself to experiment and play without judgment, trusting in the creative process to guide you toward greater self-awareness and spiritual growth.

In summary, exploring spiritual practices such as meditation, prayer, connecting with nature, and creative expression can be transformative ways to deepen your spirituality and nurture your connection to something greater than yourself. By incorporating these practices into your daily life and committing to exploring your innermost thoughts and feelings, you can cultivate a sense of peace, purpose, and fulfillment that enriches every aspect of your being. Trust in the power of these practices to support you on your spiritual journey and open yourself to the endless possibilities for growth and transformation that await.

4. How does spirituality contribute to women's sense of purpose, meaning, and inner peace?

Spirituality profoundly influences women's lives by providing them with a deep sense of purpose, meaning, and inner peace. Through spiritual exploration and connection to personal beliefs, women often discover a clarity that guides them towards a more profound understanding of their existence. This understanding transcends the routine aspects of life, offering them a sense of fulfillment that enriches every facet of their being. By fostering a connection with their inner selves and the divine, women find comfort and direction in navigating life's complexities.

To embark on a journey of spiritual discovery, it's essential to begin with self-reflection and introspection. Allocate regular time for journaling, meditation, or quiet contemplation to delve into your beliefs, values, and aspirations. These practices offer valuable insight into what truly matters to you and provide a foundation for further exploration. Embrace spiritual practices such as meditation, prayer, or spending time in nature to nurture your connection to the divine. By integrating these practices into your daily routine, you create space for introspection and spiritual growth, allowing for a deeper understanding of yourself and the world around you.

Seek out opportunities for further exploration by attending workshops, retreats, or gatherings focused on spirituality. Engaging with like-minded individuals and supportive communities can provide guidance and encouragement along your spiritual journey. These interactions offer valuable insights and perspectives that can enrich your understanding of spirituality. Finally, express your spirituality through creative outlets such as art, music, or writing. Allow your intuition and inner wisdom to guide you as you explore different avenues of self-expression. Through these actions, cultivate a deeper sense of purpose, meaning, and inner peace that resonates with your soul.

In summary, spirituality holds the power to fill women's lives with a profound sense of purpose, meaning, and inner peace. Through self-reflection, engagement with spiritual practices, seeking opportunities for growth, and creative expression, women can embark on a journey of spiritual discovery. By nurturing a connection with their inner selves and the divine, they find clarity and direction that transcends the challenges of everyday life. This journey allows women to cultivate a deeper understanding of themselves and the world around them, ultimately leading to a more fulfilling and enriched existence.

5. What role do rituals, ceremonies, and traditions play in women's spiritual journeys?

Rituals, ceremonies, and traditions serve as integral components of women's spiritual journeys, providing structure, meaning, and connection to the divine. These practices offer a sacred space for women to honor their beliefs, express gratitude, and celebrate milestones in their lives. By participating in rituals and ceremonies, women can deepen their connection to their spiritual beliefs and community, fostering a sense of belonging and interconnectedness.

To incorporate rituals, ceremonies, and traditions into your spiritual journey, begin by exploring the practices that resonate with you on a personal level. Reflect on your cultural heritage, familial traditions, and spiritual beliefs to identify rituals and ceremonies that hold significance for you. Consider attending community gatherings, workshops, or retreats focused on spiritual practices to learn more about different traditions and how they can enrich your spiritual journey.

Create opportunities to incorporate rituals and ceremonies into your daily life and special occasions. Establish simple rituals, such as lighting a candle, saying a prayer, or setting intentions, to mark the beginning or end of each day. Celebrate significant milestones, such as birthdays, weddings, or transitions, with meaningful ceremonies that reflect your spiritual beliefs and values. By infusing these practices into your life, you can cultivate a deeper sense of connection to the divine and create moments of reverence and reflection.

Honor the traditions passed down through generations while also allowing space for personalization and adaptation. Embrace the rituals and ceremonies that resonate with your soul, while also being open to creating new traditions that reflect your unique spiritual journey. By embracing rituals, ceremonies, and traditions, you can enrich your spiritual practice and deepen your connection to something greater than yourself.

6.   How can women overcome obstacles or doubts on their spiritual paths?

Obstacles and doubts are natural parts of the spiritual journey, but they need not hinder your progress. Firstly, acknowledge and embrace these challenges as opportunities for growth and self-discovery. Understand that doubts are a normal part of the journey and do not signify failure or inadequacy. Instead, view them as invitations to delve deeper into your beliefs and explore new perspectives.

Cultivate self-compassion and kindness towards yourself as you navigate these challenges. Practice patience and understanding, recognizing that spiritual growth is a gradual process that unfolds over time. Offer yourself grace and forgiveness when doubts arise, knowing that it's okay to question and reassess your beliefs along the way.

Seek support from like-minded individuals, mentors, or spiritual communities who can offer guidance and encouragement during times of doubt. Share your experiences openly and honestly with trusted confidants, allowing yourself to be vulnerable and receptive to their wisdom and support. By connecting with others who share similar struggles and experiences, you can gain new insights and perspectives that help you navigate your spiritual path with greater clarity and confidence.

Stay committed to your spiritual practice and continue to engage in activities that nourish your soul and deepen your connection to the divine. Set aside regular time for meditation, prayer, or reflection, and honor your innermost beliefs and values. Trust in the process of spiritual growth, knowing that every obstacle and doubt you encounter is an opportunity for greater understanding and transformation. Through these actions, you can overcome obstacles and doubts on your spiritual path and emerge stronger, wiser, and more aligned with your true self.

7. **How does spirituality intersect with other aspects of holistic living, such as self-care, relationships, and social justice?**

Spirituality intersects with other aspects of holistic living in profound ways, influencing how we care for ourselves, relate to others, and engage with the world around us. Firstly, spirituality informs our approach to self-care by emphasizing the importance of nurturing our inner selves and prioritizing practices that promote holistic well-being. Through spiritual practices such as meditation, prayer, or connecting with nature, we cultivate a deeper sense of self-awareness and inner peace, which forms the foundation of our self-care routines.

In our relationships, spirituality encourages us to approach interactions with compassion, empathy, and respect. By recognizing the divine spark within ourselves and others, we foster deeper connections based on understanding and acceptance. Spiritual teachings often emphasize the values of love, kindness, and forgiveness, which guide us in building healthy and fulfilling relationships that honor the sacredness of each individual.

Spirituality motivates us to advocate for social justice and equality, recognizing that all beings are interconnected and deserving of dignity and respect. By aligning our actions with our spiritual beliefs, we work towards creating a more just and compassionate society where everyone has the opportunity to thrive. This may involve participating in activism, supporting marginalized communities, or speaking out against injustice in whatever ways feel authentic and meaningful to us.

To integrate spirituality into holistic living, begin by incorporating spiritual practices into your self-care routine. Dedicate time each day to activities such as meditation, journaling, or spending time in nature to nurture your inner well-being and cultivate a sense of peace and balance. Next, approach your relationships with compassion, empathy, and openness, recognizing the divine within yourself and others. Foster deeper connections based on understanding and acceptance, fostering healthy and fulfilling relationships that honor the sacredness of each individual. Additionally, engage in acts of social justice and advocacy that align with your spiritual values, whether through volunteering, donating to causes you believe in, or using your voice to speak out against injustice. Reflect on how spirituality informs your approach to holistic living and identify ways to further integrate spiritual principles into your daily life, creating a more meaningful and fulfilling existence that honors the interconnectedness of all beings.

8. How does embracing spirituality contribute to women's overall well-being and sense of fulfillment?

Embracing spirituality can have profound effects on women's overall well-being and sense of fulfillment. By connecting with their inner selves and the divine, women often experience a deep sense of peace, purpose, and meaning in their lives. Spiritual practices such as meditation, prayer, or spending time in nature provide opportunities for introspection and self-reflection, allowing women to cultivate a greater sense of self-awareness and inner peace. Furthermore, spirituality encourages women to live in alignment with their values and beliefs, fostering a sense of authenticity and integrity in their actions and decisions.

Taking steps to incorporate spiritual practices into your daily life can contribute to your overall well-being and sense of fulfillment. Begin by setting aside regular time for meditation, prayer, or quiet reflection to nurture your connection to the divine and cultivate inner peace. Engage in activities that bring you joy and fulfillment, whether it's spending time in nature, creating art, or volunteering in your community. By aligning your actions with your spiritual beliefs and values, you can create a more meaningful and fulfilling life that honors the sacredness of each moment.

Seeking support from spiritual communities or mentors can also enhance your spiritual journey and contribute to your overall well-being. Connect with like-minded individuals who share your spiritual interests and beliefs, whether through local groups, online forums, or spiritual organizations. Engage in meaningful conversations, share experiences, and seek guidance from those who have walked a similar path. By surrounding yourself with supportive and encouraging individuals, you can find strength, inspiration, and guidance as you navigate your spiritual journey.

Ultimately, embracing spirituality is a deeply personal and transformative journey that can lead to greater well-being and fulfillment in all aspects of life. By cultivating a deeper connection to your inner self and the divine, living in alignment with your values and beliefs, and seeking support from spiritual communities, you can experience profound growth, healing, and fulfillment on your spiritual path.

Chapter 8

Relationships and Connection

1. How do relationships and social connections impact women's holistic well-being?

Relationships and social connections play a crucial role in women's holistic well-being, influencing their physical, emotional, and mental health. Meaningful connections with family, friends, and communities provide a sense of belonging, support, and validation, which are essential for overall well-being. Engaging in positive relationships fosters feelings of love, acceptance, and security, promoting emotional resilience and buffering against stress and adversity. Furthermore, social connections offer opportunities for personal growth, learning, and self-discovery, as interactions with others provide new perspectives, insights, and experiences.

Taking proactive steps to nurture and strengthen relationships is essential for women's holistic well-being. Start by prioritizing quality time with loved ones and making an effort to stay connected, whether through regular phone calls, visits, or virtual meet-ups. Actively listen to others, show empathy and understanding, and express appreciation for their presence in your life. By fostering open and honest communication, you can deepen your connections and cultivate a sense of intimacy and trust in your relationships.

Engaging in social activities and participating in community events can also enhance women's holistic well-being by promoting a sense of belonging and connection to something larger than themselves. Get involved in groups, clubs, or organizations that align with your interests and values, and seek out opportunities for collaboration, shared experiences, and collective action. By contributing to your community and supporting others, you can cultivate a sense of purpose and fulfillment, while also strengthening your social bonds and networks.

Prioritize self-care and boundaries in your relationships to ensure that they remain healthy and balanced. Take time for yourself to recharge and rejuvenate, and set boundaries to protect your emotional and mental well-being. Communicate your needs and limits clearly and assertively, and surround yourself with individuals who respect and support your boundaries. By prioritizing self-care and healthy boundaries, you can cultivate relationships that are nourishing, supportive, and conducive to your holistic well-being.

2. Some characteristics of healthy, supportive relationships, and how can women cultivate them

Healthy, supportive relationships are characterized by several key qualities that contribute to mutual growth, understanding, and well-being. Firstly, open and honest communication is essential, allowing individuals to express their thoughts, feelings, and needs openly and respectfully. Cultivating active listening skills and practicing empathy and understanding fosters deeper connections and strengthens emotional bonds. Additionally, trust and mutual respect form the foundation of healthy relationships, creating a safe space where individuals feel valued, appreciated, and accepted for who they are.

To cultivate healthy, supportive relationships, it's important to prioritize communication and emotional connection. Make time for meaningful conversations with loved ones, where you can share openly and honestly and listen attentively to their perspectives and experiences. Practice empathy and validation, acknowledging and validating each other's feelings and experiences without judgment or criticism. By fostering a culture of openness, trust, and respect, you can create a supportive environment where individuals feel safe and valued.

Another crucial aspect of healthy relationships is maintaining boundaries and practicing self-care. Set clear boundaries to protect your emotional and mental well-being, and communicate them assertively and compassionately with others. Respect and honor the boundaries of your loved ones as well, recognizing and valuing their need for autonomy and self-expression. Prioritize self-care practices that nourish and rejuvenate you, allowing you to show up fully present and engaged in your relationships.

Strive to cultivate gratitude and appreciation in your relationships, expressing gratitude for the presence and contributions of your loved ones regularly. Celebrate each other's successes and milestones, and offer support and encouragement during times of challenge or adversity. By nurturing a culture of appreciation and support, you can foster stronger bonds and create a sense of belonging and connection in your relationships.

3. How can women navigate challenging relationships and conflicts in a holistic and constructive manner?

Navigating challenging relationships and conflicts in a holistic and constructive manner requires patience, empathy, and effective communication. Begin by approaching the situation with an open mind and a willingness to understand the perspectives and feelings of all parties involved. Practice active listening, seeking to understand the underlying emotions and needs driving the conflict, and validate the experiences of others with empathy and compassion. By acknowledging each other's feelings and perspectives, you can lay the groundwork for constructive dialogue and resolution.

When faced with conflict, it's essential to communicate assertively and respectfully, expressing your thoughts, feelings, and needs clearly and honestly. Use "I" statements to express how the situation is affecting you personally, focusing on your own experiences rather than blaming or criticizing the other person. Be open to feedback and willing to compromise, seeking mutually beneficial solutions that address the needs and concerns of both parties. By engaging in open and respectful communication, you can create a safe space for dialogue and collaboration, paving the way for resolution and reconciliation.

It's important to practice self-care and boundary-setting during challenging times in relationships. Take time for self-reflection and introspection, identifying your own needs, triggers, and boundaries in the situation. Set clear and healthy boundaries to protect your emotional and mental well-being, communicating them assertively and compassionately with others. Prioritize self-care practices that nourish and rejuvenate you, allowing you to approach the conflict from a place of clarity and strength.

Seek support from trusted friends, family members, or professionals who can offer guidance and perspective during challenging times in relationships. Reach out for assistance when needed, whether through therapy, mediation, or counseling, to help facilitate constructive dialogue and resolution. By engaging in holistic practices that prioritize empathy, communication, self-care, and support, you can navigate challenging relationships and conflicts in a constructive and transformative manner, fostering growth, understanding, and healing for all involved.

4. What role does communication play in fostering meaningful connections with others?

Communication plays a pivotal role in fostering meaningful connections with others, serving as the foundation for building trust, understanding, and intimacy in relationships. Effective communication involves not only expressing thoughts and feelings but also actively listening and empathizing with others' perspectives. By engaging in open and honest dialogue, individuals can share their experiences, beliefs, and emotions, creating a deeper sense of connection and mutual understanding. Through communication, individuals can build bridges of empathy and compassion, strengthening bonds and fostering a sense of belonging and support.

To foster meaningful connections through communication, it's essential to prioritize active listening and empathy. Practice being fully present and attentive during conversations, suspending judgment and preconceived notions to truly understand the other person's perspective. Validate their experiences and emotions with empathy and compassion, demonstrating that you value and respect their feelings. By listening actively and empathizing with others' experiences, you can create a safe and supportive space for meaningful connection and understanding to flourish.

Effective communication involves expressing oneself authentically and assertively. Share your thoughts, feelings, and needs openly and honestly, using "I" statements to take ownership of your experiences and perspectives. Be transparent and vulnerable, allowing yourself to be seen and heard authentically by others. By expressing yourself assertively and authentically, you invite deeper connections and mutual understanding, fostering trust and intimacy in your relationships.

Cultivate communication skills through practice and self-awareness, seeking opportunities to engage in meaningful conversations and interactions with others. Reflect on your communication style and patterns, identifying areas for growth and improvement. Practice active listening, empathy, and assertiveness in your daily interactions, striving to create an environment of openness, respect, and trust. By honing your communication skills and fostering meaningful connections with others, you can enrich your relationships and cultivate a deeper sense of connection and fulfillment in your life.

5. How can women set boundaries and prioritize their own needs within relationships without compromising their well-being?

Setting boundaries and prioritizing one's own needs within relationships is crucial for maintaining well-being and fostering healthy connections with others. Start by identifying your values, priorities, and personal boundaries, reflecting on what you need to feel respected, supported, and fulfilled in your relationships. Communicate your boundaries assertively and compassionately with others, expressing your needs and limits clearly and respectfully. Remember that setting boundaries is not about controlling or changing others' behavior but rather about taking responsibility for your own well-being and honoring your needs and values.

Practice self-awareness and self-advocacy, tuning into your emotions and intuition to recognize when your boundaries are being crossed or compromised. Trust yourself and your instincts, and honor your feelings and needs without guilt or shame. Be firm and consistent in upholding your boundaries, even if it means saying no or asserting yourself in difficult situations. By prioritizing your own well-being and honoring your boundaries, you send a powerful message to others that your needs are valid and deserving of respect.

Prioritize self-care practices that nourish and replenish your physical, emotional, and mental well-being. Make time for activities that bring you joy, relaxation, and fulfillment, whether it's practicing mindfulness, engaging in hobbies, or spending time with loved ones. Invest in activities that support your overall well-being and help you recharge and rejuvenate, allowing you to show up fully present and engaged in your relationships.

Seek support from trusted friends, family members, or professionals who can offer guidance and perspective as you navigate setting boundaries and prioritizing your needs within relationships. Surround yourself with individuals who respect and support your boundaries, and lean on your support network for encouragement and validation. By seeking support and guidance from others, you can gain valuable insights, perspective, and encouragement as you prioritize your well-being and cultivate healthy, fulfilling relationships.

6. How do online relationships and social media impact women's sense of connection and community?

Online relationships and social media platforms can have both positive and negative impacts on women's sense of connection and community. On one hand, these digital spaces provide opportunities for women to connect with others from diverse backgrounds and geographic locations, fostering a sense of belonging and community. Through online forums, social media groups, and virtual communities, women can find support, camaraderie, and shared experiences, breaking down barriers of isolation and providing a sense of connection in an increasingly digital world.

It's important to recognize the potential downsides of online relationships and social media use. Excessive reliance on digital communication can lead to feelings of disconnection and superficiality, as interactions may lack the depth and intimacy of face-to-face connections. Moreover, the curated nature of social media platforms can contribute to comparison and self-doubt, as individuals may feel pressure to present an idealized version of themselves online, leading to feelings of inadequacy or insecurity.

To navigate the impact of online relationships and social media on their sense of connection and community, women can take proactive steps to cultivate a healthy digital presence. This may involve setting boundaries around social media use, such as limiting screen time or unfollowing accounts that trigger negative emotions. Additionally, prioritize quality over quantity in online interactions, focusing on building genuine connections with like-minded individuals rather than seeking validation or approval from a large audience.

Engaging in meaningful online communities and forums that align with your interests and values can also enhance your sense of connection and belonging. Seek out virtual spaces where you feel valued, supported, and understood, and actively participate in conversations and discussions that resonate with you. By fostering authentic connections and engaging in meaningful dialogue online, you can cultivate a sense of community and belonging that transcends the digital realm, enriching your overall sense of connection and well-being.

7. How can women cultivate empathy, compassion, and understanding in their interactions with others?

Cultivating empathy, compassion, and understanding in interactions with others is a powerful way for women to deepen their connections and foster positive relationships. Begin by practicing empathetic listening and seeking to understand the perspectives and experiences of others without judgment or bias. This involves tuning in to both verbal and nonverbal cues, empathizing with the emotions underlying their words, and validating their feelings with compassion and empathy. By empathetic listening, women can create a safe and supportive space for others to express themselves authentically and feel heard and understood.

Another way to cultivate empathy and compassion is by putting yourself in others' shoes and considering their perspectives and experiences from their point of view. This requires stepping outside of your own worldview and embracing a mindset of openness and curiosity, seeking to understand the complexities of others' lives and experiences. By practicing perspective-taking and empathy, women can develop a deeper appreciation for the diversity of human experiences and foster greater compassion and understanding in their interactions with others.

Women can cultivate compassion through acts of kindness, generosity, and service toward others. Look for opportunities to extend a helping hand, offer support, or lend a listening ear to those in need. Whether it's volunteering for a cause you care about, offering words of encouragement to a friend in distress, or simply showing kindness and empathy in your daily interactions, small gestures of compassion can have a profound impact on others' well-being and contribute to a more empathetic and caring society.

Prioritize self-reflection and personal growth in your journey toward cultivating empathy, compassion, and understanding. Take time to reflect on your own biases, assumptions, and blind spots, and challenge yourself to expand your perspective and deepen your empathy for others. Engage in practices such as journaling, mindfulness, or self-awareness exercises to enhance your capacity for empathy and compassion, and commit to ongoing learning and growth in this area. By fostering empathy, compassion, and understanding in your interactions with others, you can cultivate deeper connections, foster positive relationships, and contribute to a more empathetic and compassionate world.

8. Some strategies for building and maintaining strong friendships and support networks

Building and maintaining strong friendships and support networks requires effort, intentionality, and mutual investment from all parties involved. Start by actively seeking out opportunities to connect with others who share your interests, values, and passions. This might involve joining clubs, organizations, or community groups where you can meet like-minded individuals and forge meaningful connections based on shared experiences and interests. Additionally, prioritize quality over quantity in your friendships, focusing on cultivating a few close, trusted relationships rather than spreading yourself too thin across many superficial connections.

Once you've established friendships, invest time and energy into nurturing and maintaining them. Make a conscious effort to stay in touch with friends regularly, whether through phone calls, text messages, or in-person visits. Schedule regular get-togethers or outings to catch up and spend quality time together, and make an effort to actively listen and engage in meaningful conversations. Show appreciation for your friends and support them in both good times and bad, offering a listening ear, words of encouragement, and practical assistance when needed.

Be open to expanding your social circle and forming new connections over time. Keep an open mind and be receptive to meeting new people from diverse backgrounds and walks of life, and be proactive in initiating and maintaining connections with potential friends. Look for opportunities to participate in social activities or events where you can meet new people and forge connections based on shared interests and values.

Prioritize reciprocity and mutual support in your friendships, cultivating a culture of trust, respect, and reciprocity where both parties feel valued, supported, and understood. Be willing to offer help, support, and encouragement to your friends when they need it, and don't hesitate to reach out and ask for assistance or support when you need it yourself. By fostering strong friendships and support networks based on trust, mutual respect, and reciprocity, you can create a source of comfort, joy, and companionship in your life, enriching your overall well-being and sense of connection.

9. How does the quality of women's relationships influence their overall happiness and fulfillment?

The quality of women's relationships plays a significant role in shaping their overall happiness and fulfillment. Close, supportive relationships can provide a sense of belonging, connection, and emotional support, buffering against stress, loneliness, and adversity. When women feel understood, valued, and supported by their friends and loved ones, they experience greater levels of happiness, satisfaction, and well-being in their lives. Conversely, strained or unhealthy relationships can lead to feelings of loneliness, isolation, and dissatisfaction, undermining women's mental and emotional well-being.

To prioritize the quality of their relationships, women can focus on cultivating genuine connections based on mutual respect, trust, and empathy. Invest time and effort into nurturing close friendships and meaningful connections with loved ones, prioritizing open communication, active listening, and openness in your interactions. Be willing to show openness and authenticity in your relationships, allowing yourself to be seen and understood by others, and encourage the same openness and honesty from your friends and loved ones.

Women can also prioritize boundaries and self-care in their relationships to ensure they maintain a healthy balance between giving and receiving support. Set boundaries around your time, energy, and emotional availability, and communicate your needs and limits assertively and compassionately with others. Make time for self-care practices that nourish and replenish your well-being, and prioritize activities and relationships that bring you joy, fulfillment, and a sense of connection.

Seek out opportunities to cultivate a diverse and supportive network of relationships, including both close friends and acquaintances who offer different perspectives, experiences, and forms of support. Surround yourself with individuals who uplift and empower you, and be proactive in reaching out and offering support to others in return. By prioritizing the quality of your relationships and nurturing connections based on trust, empathy, and reciprocity, you can cultivate a rich tapestry of meaningful connections that contribute to your overall happiness and fulfillment in life.

10. How can women nurture their relationships while also prioritizing their own self-care and personal growth?

Nurturing relationships while prioritizing self-care and personal growth requires finding a balance between giving to others and attending to one's own needs. Start by practicing effective time management and boundary-setting techniques to ensure you have dedicated time for both nurturing your relationships and engaging in self-care activities. Communicate openly and honestly with your loved ones about your need for personal time and space, and encourage them to do the same. By setting clear boundaries and expectations, you can create a supportive environment where both your relationships and your well-being can thrive.

Integrate self-care practices into your daily routine to ensure you prioritize your own well-being while nurturing your relationships. This might involve carving out time each day for activities that replenish your energy and nourish your soul, such as meditation, exercise, creative pursuits, or spending time in nature. By prioritizing self-care, you can cultivate a strong foundation of personal well-being that enables you to show up fully present and engaged in your relationships, fostering deeper connections and more meaningful interactions with others.

View personal growth as a shared journey that can enhance your relationships rather than detract from them. Engage in activities that support your personal development, such as pursuing educational opportunities, exploring new interests, or seeking out experiences that challenge and inspire you. Share your journey of growth and self-discovery with your loved ones, inviting them to join you in exploring new passions, learning together, and supporting each other's aspirations. By integrating personal growth into your relationships, you can deepen your connections with others and create a sense of shared purpose and growth.

Practice self-compassion and forgiveness as you navigate the balancing act of nurturing relationships and prioritizing your own well-being. Recognize that it's normal to have moments of imbalance or to feel guilty for taking time for yourself, and be gentle with yourself as you learn to navigate these challenges. Remember that nurturing your own well-being is not selfish but rather essential for showing up as your best self in your relationships. By practicing self-compassion and forgiveness, you can cultivate a sense of inner peace and resilience that allows you to nurture your relationships from a place of authenticity and wholeness.

Chapter 9

Fertility, Pregnancy, and Motherhood

1. What are the holistic considerations for women's fertility and preconception health?

When considering fertility and preconception health from a holistic perspective, it's essential to address various physical, emotional, and lifestyle factors that can influence reproductive well-being. Start by focusing on optimizing overall health and well-being through nutritious diet, regular exercise, and adequate sleep. Incorporate nutrient-rich foods into your diet, such as fruits, vegetables, whole grains, lean proteins, and healthy fats, to support hormonal balance and reproductive function. Engage in regular physical activity to maintain a healthy weight and reduce stress, as excess weight and chronic stress can negatively impact fertility.

Prioritize emotional well-being and stress management as part of your preconception health plan. Practice stress-reduction techniques such as mindfulness, meditation, yoga, or deep breathing exercises to promote relaxation and reduce the negative effects of stress on reproductive health. Seek out support from loved ones, friends, or a mental health professional if you're experiencing emotional challenges or struggling to cope with fertility-related stressors. By prioritizing emotional well-being, you can create a supportive foundation for your fertility journey and enhance your overall sense of well-being.

Address environmental and lifestyle factors that can impact fertility and reproductive health. Minimize exposure to environmental toxins and pollutants by choosing organic foods, using natural personal care products, and avoiding harmful chemicals in your home and environment. Limit alcohol consumption, quit smoking, and avoid recreational drugs, as these substances can impair fertility and harm reproductive function. Create a supportive and nurturing environment for conception by fostering healthy habits and minimizing exposure to harmful substances.

Seek out holistic healthcare providers who can offer personalized support and guidance tailored to your individual needs and preferences. Consider working with a naturopathic doctor, fertility specialist, or holistic nutritionist who can provide evidence-based recommendations and support you in optimizing your fertility and preconception health. Collaborate with your healthcare team to develop a comprehensive preconception plan that addresses all aspects of your well-being, from nutrition and lifestyle to emotional and environmental factors. By taking a holistic approach to fertility and preconception health, you can optimize your chances of conceiving and promote overall well-being for you and your future child.

2. How can women support their reproductive health and optimize their chances of conception naturally?

Supporting reproductive health and optimizing chances of conception naturally involves a multifaceted approach that addresses various aspects of physical, emotional, and lifestyle factors. Start by focusing on maintaining a balanced and nutritious diet rich in essential nutrients such as folate, iron, zinc, and omega-3 fatty acids, which are crucial for reproductive function and hormonal balance. Incorporate a variety of fruits, vegetables, whole grains, lean proteins, and healthy fats into your meals to ensure you're meeting your nutritional needs for fertility.

Prioritize regular physical activity to support overall health and fertility. Engage in moderate-intensity exercise such as brisk walking, swimming, or cycling for at least 30 minutes most days of the week to help regulate menstrual cycles, reduce stress, and maintain a healthy weight. Avoid excessive exercise or extreme weight loss, as these can disrupt hormonal balance and impair reproductive function. Aim for a balanced approach to exercise that supports overall well-being without placing excessive strain on your body.

Prioritize emotional well-being and stress management as part of your fertility journey. Practice stress-reduction techniques such as mindfulness meditation, yoga, deep breathing exercises, or journaling to promote relaxation and reduce the negative effects of stress on reproductive health. Seek out support from loved ones, friends, or a mental health professional if you're experiencing emotional challenges or struggling to cope with fertility-related stressors. By prioritizing emotional well-being, you can create a supportive foundation for conception and enhance your overall sense of well-being.

Consider incorporating holistic therapies and practices into your fertility journey to support reproductive health and optimize chances of conception naturally. Consult with a qualified healthcare provider or holistic practitioner to discuss which therapies may be appropriate for you and develop a personalized plan that addresses your individual needs and goals. By taking a holistic approach to supporting reproductive health, you can optimize your chances of conception naturally and promote overall well-being for you and your future child.

3. Holistic approaches women can explore for managing fertility challenges and infertility.

For women facing fertility challenges and infertility, exploring holistic approaches can offer a comprehensive and supportive path towards conception. Start by seeking out a qualified healthcare provider or fertility specialist who understands and supports holistic approaches to reproductive health. Collaborate with them to develop a personalized treatment plan that integrates evidence-based medical interventions with holistic therapies and practices tailored to your individual needs and goals. By combining the best of conventional and alternative medicine, you can address the root causes of fertility challenges and optimize your chances of conception.

Prioritize lifestyle factors that support reproductive health and overall well-being. Focus on maintaining a balanced diet rich in essential nutrients, engaging in regular physical activity, managing stress, and prioritizing emotional well-being. Explore stress-reduction techniques such as mindfulness meditation, yoga, or acupuncture to promote relaxation and reduce the negative effects of stress on reproductive function. By taking a holistic approach to lifestyle factors, you can create a supportive environment for fertility and enhance your overall sense of well-being.

Cultivate a supportive network of loved ones, friends, and fellow fertility warriors who understand and empathize with your journey. Joining a support group, online community, or fertility wellness program can provide valuable emotional support, practical advice, and a sense of connection with others who are navigating similar challenges. Share your experiences, seek out information and resources, and draw strength from the collective wisdom and support of your community. By embracing a holistic approach to managing fertility challenges, you can empower yourself to take an active role in your reproductive health journey and optimize your chances of achieving your dream of conception.

4. **How does holistic prenatal care differ from conventional prenatal care, and what are its benefits**

Holistic prenatal care differs from conventional prenatal care in that it takes into account the physical, emotional, and spiritual aspects of pregnancy and childbirth. While conventional prenatal care typically focuses on medical interventions such as routine tests, screenings, and medications, holistic prenatal care emphasizes a more comprehensive approach that addresses the whole person. This may include nutritional counseling, personalized exercise plans, stress reduction techniques, emotional support, and complementary therapies.

One of the key benefits of holistic prenatal care is its emphasis on empowering women to take an active role in their own health and well-being during pregnancy. Rather than simply relying on medical professionals to manage their care, women are encouraged to become partners in the process, making informed decisions about their health and advocating for their own needs and preferences. This collaborative approach fosters a sense of empowerment, confidence, and autonomy, allowing women to feel more in control of their pregnancy and childbirth experiences.

Another advantage of holistic prenatal care is its focus on promoting optimal health and wellness for both mother and baby. By addressing factors such as nutrition, stress management, and emotional well-being, holistic care aims to create the ideal conditions for a healthy pregnancy, smooth labor and delivery, and positive outcomes for both mother and baby. This proactive approach to prenatal care can help prevent complications, reduce the risk of medical interventions, and support the body's natural ability to nurture and sustain new life.

Holistic prenatal care often incorporates complementary and alternative therapies that can complement conventional medical treatments and enhance overall well-being. Modalities such as relaxation techniques can help alleviate common pregnancy discomforts, reduce stress, and promote relaxation and emotional balance. By integrating these holistic therapies into prenatal care, women can experience a more holistic and supportive approach to pregnancy that addresses their physical, emotional, and spiritual needs throughout the journey to motherhood.

5. How can women prepare for childbirth holistically, including exploring options for natural birth and informed decision-making?

Preparing for childbirth holistically involves taking a proactive approach to educate yourself about the birthing process, explore various options for labor and delivery, and make informed decisions that align with your preferences and values. Start by seeking out resources and information on natural childbirth, including books, classes, and online forums that provide insights into the physiology of labor, coping techniques, and strategies for achieving a positive birth experience.

Trust your body's innate wisdom and ability to give birth, and embrace the journey of childbirth with an open heart and mind. Stay flexible and adaptable to the unpredictable nature of labor and delivery, and approach childbirth as a transformative and empowering experience that will usher you into motherhood with strength and confidence. By preparing for childbirth holistically and making informed decisions that honor your individual needs and preferences, you can approach labor and delivery with a sense of empowerment, trust, and readiness to welcome your baby into the world.

6. Some holistic approaches to postpartum recovery and adjusting to motherhood

Transitioning into motherhood and navigating the postpartum period can be a profound and transformative experience, both physically and emotionally. Embracing holistic approaches to postpartum recovery can support your healing journey and help you adjust to the demands of new motherhood. Start by prioritizing rest and self-care in the early weeks and months after childbirth. Allow yourself ample time to recover from labor and birth, and listen to your body's cues to rest, nourish, and replenish your energy levels. Create a supportive postpartum care plan that includes adequate rest, nutritious meals, and assistance with household tasks to promote healing and recovery.

Focus on nurturing your emotional well-being and adjusting to the emotional challenges of motherhood. Seek out emotional support from your partner, family members, friends, and healthcare providers, and openly communicate your feelings and concerns about the postpartum period. Joining a new mother's support group or participating in online forums can provide valuable peer support, encouragement, and validation as you navigate the highs and lows of early motherhood. Practice self-compassion and patience with yourself as you adjust to your new role as a mother, and allow yourself grace and acceptance during this transitional period.

Explore holistic therapies and practices that promote postpartum healing and emotional wellness. Consider incorporating gentle movement practices such as postpartum yoga, walking, or stretching exercises to promote circulation, reduce muscle tension, and improve mood. Treat yourself to nurturing self-care rituals such as warm baths, massage, or aromatherapy to promote relaxation and reduce stress. Explore holistic modalities such as acupuncture, herbal remedies, or postpartum doula support to address specific postpartum concerns such as breastfeeding challenges, hormonal imbalances, or mood disorders.

Prioritize bonding and connection with your baby through skin-to-skin contact, breastfeeding, baby wearing, and responsive caregiving practices that promote secure attachment and emotional bonding. Allow yourself time to savor and cherish the precious moments of early motherhood, and trust in your instincts as you navigate the joys and challenges of caring for your newborn. By embracing holistic approaches to postpartum recovery and adjusting to motherhood, you can nurture your physical and emotional well-being and lay a strong foundation for a healthy and fulfilling journey into parenthood.

7. How can women prioritize self-care and mental health during the transition to motherhood?

Transitioning to motherhood is a monumental life change that can bring joy, fulfillment, and also challenges. Prioritizing self-care and mental health during this transition is crucial for maintaining your well-being and navigating the ups and downs of early motherhood. Start by acknowledging the importance of self-care and making it a non-negotiable part of your daily routine. Set aside dedicated time each day for activities that nourish your body, mind, and spirit, whether it's taking a warm bath, practicing mindfulness meditation, or indulging in a hobby you love.

Prioritize mental health by seeking out professional support if needed. The postpartum period can bring about a range of emotions, from joy and excitement to anxiety and overwhelm. If you're struggling with feelings of sadness, anxiety, or depression, don't hesitate to reach out to a therapist, counselor, or mental health professional who specializes in perinatal mental health. Talking to a trained professional can provide you with coping strategies, emotional support, and validation for your experiences, helping you navigate the emotional challenges of new motherhood with greater resilience and confidence.

Cultivate a strong support network of friends, family members, and fellow mothers who understand and empathize with the unique demands of early motherhood. Surround yourself with people who uplift and encourage you, and don't hesitate to lean on them for practical help, emotional support, and reassurance when needed. Joining a new mother's group, attending breastfeeding support meetings, or participating in online forums can also provide you with valuable peer support, camaraderie, and a sense of community during this transitional period.

Practice self-compassion and let go of unrealistic expectations of motherhood. It's normal to experience a range of emotions and challenges as you adjust to your new role as a mother, and it's okay to not have all the answers or to feel overwhelmed at times. Give yourself permission to prioritize your own needs and well-being, and remember that taking care of yourself is essential for being the best parent you can be to your baby. By prioritizing self-care and mental health during the transition to motherhood, you can cultivate greater resilience, confidence, and emotional well-being as you embark on this transformative journey.

8. What role do partners, family, and community support play in women's experiences of fertility, pregnancy, and motherhood?

Partners, family, and community support play integral roles in women's experiences of fertility, pregnancy, and motherhood, providing invaluable emotional, practical, and social support throughout each stage of the journey. During the fertility journey, partners can offer understanding, encouragement, and solidarity as couples navigate the challenges of conception. Open communication and mutual support within the partnership can help alleviate stress and foster a sense of teamwork and shared responsibility. Additionally, family members and friends can provide emotional support and empathy, offering a listening ear, words of encouragement, and reassurance during times of uncertainty or disappointment.

Throughout pregnancy, partners, family, and community support continue to play crucial roles in women's experiences. Partners can actively participate in prenatal appointments, childbirth education classes, and birth planning discussions, demonstrating their commitment to the pregnancy journey and fostering a sense of partnership and shared decision-making. Family members and friends can offer practical assistance, such as helping with household tasks, providing transportation to appointments, or preparing meals, easing the burden on expectant mothers and promoting a sense of care and support.

As women transition into motherhood, partners, family, and community support become even more essential. Partners can offer hands-on assistance with newborn care, diaper changes, and feeding responsibilities, allowing mothers to rest and recover from childbirth. Family members and friends can provide emotional support and encouragement, offering a listening ear, practical advice, and reassurance during the challenges of early motherhood. Additionally, community resources such as new mother support groups, lactation consultants, and postpartum doulas can offer valuable guidance, camaraderie, and validation as women navigate the joys and struggles of caring for a newborn.

In cultivating a supportive network of partners, family, and community, women can enhance their experiences of fertility, pregnancy, and motherhood, fostering a sense of belonging, connection, and resilience. Partners can commit to being active participants in the journey, offering understanding, empathy, and practical assistance at every step. Family members and friends can provide unconditional love, support, and encouragement, serving as pillars of strength and solidarity during times of joy and challenge. By nurturing these relationships and seeking out community resources, women can feel empowered, supported, and uplifted as they navigate the transformative journey of fertility, pregnancy, and motherhood.

9. How can women embrace the holistic journey of motherhood, nurturing themselves and their families with love and intention?

Embracing the holistic journey of motherhood involves nurturing oneself and one's family with love, mindfulness, and intentionality. Start by prioritizing self-care and well-being, recognizing that taking care of yourself is essential for nurturing your family effectively.

In addition to self-care, cultivate a nurturing and intentional family environment by creating rituals and traditions that foster connection, meaning, and joy. Whether it's sharing meals together, engaging in family outings, or setting aside time for storytelling or creative activities, prioritize quality time spent together as a family. Embrace the opportunity to create memories and traditions that reflect your family's values and bring you closer together, strengthening the bonds of love and connection that sustain you through life's ups and downs.

Practice mindfulness and presence in your interactions with your children, partner, and other loved ones, savoring the precious moments of parenthood and cultivating gratitude for the blessings in your life. Slow down and cherish the simple pleasures of everyday life, whether it's watching your child play, sharing laughter around the dinner table, or enjoying a cozy cuddle before bedtime. By cultivating a mindful and present approach to motherhood, you can deepen your connection with your family and experience greater fulfillment and joy in the journey of parenting.

Prioritize open communication and mutual support within your family unit, creating a safe and nurturing environment where everyone feels valued, heard, and supported. Foster honest and loving communication with your partner and children, expressing your needs, feelings, and concerns openly and respectfully. Encourage a spirit of cooperation, empathy, and understanding, and embrace the opportunity to learn and grow together as a family. By nurturing yourself and your family with love and intention, you can embrace the holistic journey of motherhood with grace, authenticity, and joy.

Chapter 10

Empowerment and Self-Expression

1. What does empowerment mean for women, and why is it important for holistic living?

Empowerment for women encompasses a multifaceted concept that involves gaining confidence, autonomy, and agency in various aspects of life. It entails recognizing and asserting one's rights, abilities, and choices, enabling women to pursue their goals, fulfill their potential, and advocate for themselves and others. Empowerment is essential for holistic living because it fosters a sense of self-worth, resilience, and purpose, empowering women to take ownership of their health, well-being, and overall quality of life. By cultivating a mindset of empowerment, women can embrace a holistic approach to living that prioritizes self-care, personal growth, and meaningful engagement with the world around them.

To cultivate empowerment in your own life, start by identifying your strengths, values, and aspirations, and setting clear and achievable goals that align with your vision for holistic living. Take steps to develop self-confidence and assertiveness, whether it's through affirmations, positive self-talk, or seeking out opportunities for personal and professional growth. Surround yourself with supportive and empowering influences, including mentors, friends, and role models who uplift and inspire you to reach your full potential.

Advocate for yourself and others by speaking up for what you believe in, challenging societal norms and stereotypes, and promoting gender equality and social justice in your community and beyond. Take ownership of your health and well-being by prioritizing self-care practices that nurture your body, mind, and spirit, such as regular exercise, healthy eating, mindfulness meditation, and stress management techniques.

Support and uplift other women in their journeys toward empowerment, recognizing that collective action and solidarity are essential for creating meaningful and lasting change. Whether it's through mentorship, volunteering, or participating in advocacy initiatives, find ways to contribute to the empowerment of women in your community and amplify their voices and experiences. By embracing empowerment as a guiding principle in your life, you can cultivate a sense of agency, resilience, and fulfillment that supports your holistic well-being and contributes to positive change in the world.

2. How can women cultivate self-confidence, self-esteem, and a sense of agency in their lives?

Cultivating self-confidence, self-esteem, and a sense of agency is essential for women to navigate life with resilience, authenticity, and purpose. Start by acknowledging your strengths, talents, and accomplishments, recognizing that you possess unique qualities and abilities that contribute to your worth and potential. Challenge negative self-talk and limiting beliefs that undermine your confidence, replacing them with affirmations and positive reframes that reinforce your value and capabilities.

Take proactive steps to invest in your personal growth and development, whether it's through learning new skills, pursuing hobbies and interests, or seeking out opportunities for education and self-improvement. Set achievable goals that push you outside your comfort zone and allow you to stretch and grow, celebrating your progress and achievements along the way. By continuously challenging yourself and expanding your horizons, you can build confidence and self-assurance that empowers you to navigate life's challenges with grace and resilience.

Cultivate a supportive and nurturing environment that fosters your self-esteem and sense of agency. Surround yourself with people who uplift and encourage you, fostering positive relationships that affirm your worth and potential. Seek out mentors, role models, and peers who inspire and empower you, providing guidance, support, and perspective as you navigate your journey of self-discovery and personal growth.

Embrace opportunities for self-expression and advocacy, using your voice and talents to advocate for your needs, values, and aspirations. Take ownership of your choices and decisions, trusting in your intuition and wisdom to guide you toward paths that align with your authentic self and purpose. By embracing self-confidence, self-esteem, and a sense of agency, you can cultivate a deep sense of empowerment that fuels your holistic well-being and enables you to thrive in all areas of your life.

3. What are some common barriers to women's empowerment, and how can they be overcome?

Navigating the journey toward empowerment, women may encounter various barriers that hinder their progress and limit their opportunities for growth and fulfillment. One common barrier is societal expectations and stereotypes that impose narrow definitions of femininity and success, constraining women's sense of identity and potential. To overcome this barrier, challenge gender norms and stereotypes by embracing your authentic self and celebrating the diversity of women's experiences and achievements. Reject limiting beliefs and expectations that do not serve your growth and well-being, empowering yourself to define success on your own terms.

Another barrier to women's empowerment is systemic discrimination and inequality, which disproportionately impact marginalized communities and limit access to resources, opportunities, and representation. Addressing systemic barriers requires collective action and advocacy to dismantle oppressive structures and create more equitable and inclusive systems. Get involved in grassroots movements, advocacy initiatives, and community organizations that work toward gender equality and social justice, amplifying marginalized voices and supporting for policy changes that promote equal rights and opportunities for all.

Internalized sexism and self-doubt can serve as significant barriers to women's empowerment, undermining their confidence, self-esteem, and sense of agency. Combatting internalized oppression involves cultivating self-awareness, self-compassion, and self-acceptance, recognizing and challenging the negative beliefs and attitudes that undermine your confidence and potential. Practice self-care and mindfulness techniques that nurture your mental and emotional well-being, fostering a positive self-image and resilient mindset that empowers you to overcome self-doubt and pursue your goals with confidence and determination.

Lack of access to education, economic opportunities, and supportive networks can pose significant barriers to women's empowerment, particularly in resource-constrained environments. To address these challenges, advocate for increased access to education, vocational training, and economic resources that empower women to pursue their aspirations and achieve financial independence. Build supportive networks and alliances with other women and supporters who share your goals and values, collaborating to overcome barriers and create pathways to empowerment for all. By identifying and addressing these barriers to empowerment, you can cultivate a more inclusive and equitable world where all women have the opportunity to thrive and fulfill their potential.

4. How does self-expression contribute to women's holistic well-being and personal fulfillment?

Self-expression plays a crucial role in enhancing women's holistic well-being and fostering personal fulfillment by providing a means of authentic communication and creative exploration. Through self-expression, women can articulate their thoughts, feelings, and experiences, fostering a deeper understanding and acceptance of themselves. By expressing their unique identities, perspectives, and emotions, women cultivate a sense of authenticity and self-awareness that promotes mental and emotional well-being. Engaging in creative outlets (hobbies) such as writing, art, music, or dance allows women to tap into their inner creativity and imagination, fostering a sense of joy, fulfillment, and connection to their innermost selves.

To harness the power of self-expression in your life, explore different creative outlets and find activities that resonate with your interests and passions. Whether it's journaling, painting, singing, or dancing, experiment with different forms of expression to discover what brings you joy and fulfillment. Set aside dedicated time for creative pursuits in your daily or weekly routine, prioritizing self-expression as a vital aspect of your holistic well-being. Create a supportive and nurturing environment that encourages open and honest expression, whether it's through engaging with like-minded individuals, joining creative communities or workshops, or sharing your work with trusted friends or mentors.

Use self-expression as a tool for self-discovery and personal growth, allowing yourself to explore and express your thoughts, emotions, and aspirations without judgment or embarrassment. Embrace openness and authenticity in your creative actions, recognizing that true self-expression requires courage and openness. Reflect on your experiences and insights gained through creative expression, recognizing the ways in which self-expression enriches your life and contributes to your overall sense of fulfillment and well-being. By embracing self-expression as a fundamental aspect of your holistic journey, you can cultivate a deeper connection to yourself, others, and the world around you, fostering a sense of purpose, meaning, and personal fulfillment in your life.

5. What are some creative outlets and forms of self-expression that women can explore?

Women have a countless of creative outlets and forms of self-expression to explore, each offering unique opportunities for personal growth, fulfillment, and connection. Writing is a versatile and accessible outlet that allows women to express their thoughts, emotions, and experiences through journals, poetry, fiction, or personal essays. Consider setting aside time each day or week to write freely, exploring your innermost thoughts and feelings without judgment. Joining a writing group or workshop can provide a supportive community and valuable feedback, helping you refine your craft and cultivate your voice as a writer.

Visual arts such as painting, drawing, or photography offer another avenue for self-expression, allowing women to capture and convey their perspectives, emotions, and imaginations through imagery and symbolism. Experiment with different mediums and techniques to find what resonates with you, whether it's watercolors, acrylics, or digital photography. Dedicate regular sessions to creating art, whether it's in a dedicated studio space or simply at your kitchen table, allowing yourself to immerse in the creative process and explore your unique artistic vision.

Music and dance provide powerful forms of self-expression that engage the body, mind, and spirit, offering women a dynamic outlet for emotional release, creativity, and connection. Explore your musical talents through singing, playing an instrument, or composing your own music, experimenting with different genres and styles that speak to your soul. Similarly, dance offers a rhythmic and embodied form of expression that allows women to connect with their bodies and emotions, whether through structured dance classes, spontaneous movement, or freestyle expression in the privacy of their homes.

Crafting and DIY projects provide hands-on opportunities for self-expression and creativity, allowing women to channel their energy into making tangible objects that reflect their personality and interests. From knitting and sewing to woodworking and pottery, there are endless possibilities for exploring your creativity and expressing yourself through crafting. Set aside time to engage in crafting projects that inspire you, whether it's making handmade gifts for loved ones, decorating your living space, or simply enjoying the process of creating something with your hands.

By exploring these diverse creative outlets and forms of self-expression, women can tap into their innate creativity, cultivate a deeper connection to themselves, and experience the joy and fulfillment that comes from expressing their authentic selves. Experiment with different activities and find what resonates with you, allowing yourself the freedom to explore and discover new avenues for creative expression along your journey of self-discovery and personal growth.

6. **How can women overcome societal pressures and expectations to embrace their authentic selves?**

Overcoming societal pressures and expectations to embrace your authentic self can be a challenging but transformative journey toward self-discovery and personal empowerment. Start by cultivating self-awareness and reflection, taking the time to explore your values, beliefs, and desires independent of external influences. Journaling, meditation, or therapy can be valuable tools for deepening your understanding of yourself and identifying the ways in which societal pressures may have shaped your sense of identity and self-worth.

Challenge societal norms and expectations that do not align with your authentic self by setting boundaries and asserting your values and boundaries. Practice saying no to obligations or roles that compromise your authenticity and prioritize activities and relationships that honor and celebrate your true self. Surround yourself with supportive friends, family, and communities who accept you for who you are and encourage you to embrace your uniqueness without judgment or reservation.

Seek out role models and representation that reflect diverse identities and experiences, helping you realize that there is no one-size-fits-all definition of womanhood or success. Engage with literature, media, and art that celebrates diversity and challenges stereotypes, expanding your perspective and validating your experiences. Take inspiration from individuals who have embraced their authentic selves and forged their own paths, recognizing that authenticity and fulfillment come from living in alignment with your truth, not conforming to societal expectations.

Practice self-compassion and patience as you navigate the journey toward authenticity, recognizing that it is a process of continual growth and self-discovery. Celebrate your progress and achievements along the way, acknowledging the courage and resilience it takes to challenge societal norms and embrace your true self. By taking intentional steps to overcome societal pressures and expectations, you can cultivate a deeper sense of self-acceptance, confidence, and fulfillment, empowering yourself to live authentically and wholeheartedly as the woman you truly are.

7. Self-discovery and personal growth contribute to women's empowerment

Self-discovery and personal growth are integral aspects of women's empowerment, offering opportunities for self-awareness, confidence, and autonomy. Through self-discovery, women gain a deeper understanding of their strengths, values, and aspirations, allowing them to reclaim ownership of their lives and make empowered choices that align with their authentic selves. By exploring their interests, passions, and boundaries, women cultivate a sense of agency and self-determination, breaking free from societal expectations and limitations that may have previously constrained their potential.

To embark on a journey of self-discovery and personal growth, start by setting aside dedicated time for introspection and reflection. Engage in practices such as journaling, meditation, or self-inquiry to explore your thoughts, feelings, and experiences with curiosity and compassion. Identify areas of your life where you feel fulfilled and aligned with your authentic self, as well as areas where you may seek growth or transformation. By fostering a mindset of openness and curiosity, you can embrace the process of self-discovery as a lifelong journey of exploration and evolution.

As you deepen your self-awareness and understanding, take proactive steps to pursue personal growth and development in areas that resonate with your values and aspirations. Seek out opportunities for learning, whether through formal education, mentorship, or self-directed study, that expand your knowledge, skills, and perspectives. Surround yourself with supportive individuals who encourage and challenge you to reach your fullest potential, fostering a community of empowerment and growth.

Integrate self-care practices into your daily routine to nurture your physical, mental, and emotional well-being as you navigate the process of self-discovery and personal growth. Prioritize activities that replenish your energy and nourish your soul, whether it's spending time in nature, practicing mindfulness, or engaging in creative pursuits. By prioritizing self-care, you can cultivate resilience, balance, and inner strength, empowering yourself to face challenges and obstacles with courage and confidence.

Self-discovery and personal growth serve as catalysts for women's empowerment, empowering them to embrace their authenticity, pursue their passions, and create lives of purpose and fulfillment. By embarking on a journey of self-discovery with intention and self-compassion, you can unlock your fullest potential and embrace the transformative power of personal growth in your life.

8. The role of goal-setting, intention-setting, and visualization play in empowering women to create the lives they desire.

Goal-setting, intention-setting, and visualization are powerful tools that empower women to manifest their dreams and aspirations into reality. By setting clear and achievable goals, women can articulate their desires and aspirations, providing direction and purpose to their actions. Intention-setting allows women to align their thoughts, beliefs, and actions with their goals, harnessing the power of intention to create positive change and transformation in their lives. Visualization complements goal-setting and intention-setting by allowing women to vividly imagine themselves achieving their goals, activating their subconscious mind and inner resources to support their journey toward success.

To harness the power of goal-setting, intention-setting, and visualization in your life, start by clarifying your vision and identifying your most important goals and aspirations. Take the time to reflect on what truly matters to you and what you envision for your future, considering both short-term and long-term objectives. Write down your goals in specific, measurable, and achievable terms, ensuring clarity and focus in your intentions. By articulating your goals with precision, you can create a roadmap for success and take actionable steps toward realizing your dreams.

Infuse your goals with intention by aligning your thoughts, beliefs, and actions with your desired outcomes. Cultivate a positive mindset and affirm your belief in your ability to achieve your goals, releasing any limiting beliefs or self-doubt that may hold you back. Set intentions for how you will approach your goals with purpose, dedication, and resilience, embodying the qualities and values that support your vision for success. By infusing your goals with intention, you can tap into the power of the subconscious mind and the law of attraction to manifest your desires with greater ease and effectiveness.

Practice visualization as a powerful tool for programming your subconscious mind and creating a mental blueprint for success. Set aside time each day to visualize yourself achieving your goals with vivid detail and emotional intensity, engaging all your senses to immerse yourself in the experience of success. Visualize the steps you need to take to reach your goals, imagining yourself overcoming obstacles and celebrating milestones along the way. By consistently practicing visualization, you can reprogram your subconscious mind to support your goals and align your actions with your vision for success.

Take inspired action toward your goals by implementing a strategic action plan and committing to consistent effort and perseverance. Break down your goals into manageable tasks and create a timeline for completion, holding yourself accountable to your commitments and adjusting your approach as needed. Surround yourself with supportive individuals who believe in your potential and encourage you to stay focused and motivated on your journey. By combining goal-setting, intention-setting, and visualization with strategic action and support, you can empower yourself to create the life you desire and deserve.

9. **How can women support and uplift each other in their journeys toward empowerment and self-expression?**

Supporting and uplifting each other in the journey toward empowerment and self-expression is essential for creating a culture of solidarity and mutual growth among women. One way to do this is by cultivating a sense of sisterhood and community, where women come together to celebrate each other's successes, offer encouragement during challenges, and provide a safe space for authentic self-expression. By fostering connections based on empathy, compassion, and understanding, women can create a supportive network that uplifts and empowers each other to reach their fullest potential.

To support and uplift other women in their journeys, practice active listening and empathy, taking the time to understand their experiences, perspectives, and needs without judgment or criticism. By offering a compassionate ear and validating their feelings, you can create a sense of belonging and acceptance that encourages women to share their struggles and triumphs openly. Show genuine interest in their goals, dreams, and aspirations, offering words of encouragement and affirmation that inspire confidence and resilience.

Champion other women's achievements and successes, celebrating their accomplishments and highlighting their strengths and talents. By recognizing and amplifying each other's voices and contributions, women can combat the pervasive culture of competition and comparison, fostering an environment of collaboration and mutual support. Share stories of inspiring women who have overcome obstacles and made a positive impact in their communities, serving as role models and sources of inspiration for others to follow.

Create opportunities for mentorship and mentoring, where women can share their knowledge, skills, and experiences to support each other's personal and professional growth. Offer guidance, advice, and practical support to women who are navigating challenges or seeking guidance in their journey toward empowerment and self-expression. By paying it forward and lifting others as you climb, you contribute to a cycle of empowerment and collective upliftment that benefits everyone involved.

In conclusion, by fostering a culture of support, encouragement, and sisterhood, women can uplift and empower each other in their journeys toward empowerment and self-expression. Through active listening, celebration of achievements, mentorship, and community-building initiatives, women can create a nurturing and empowering environment where everyone has the opportunity to thrive and succeed. Together, we can amplify each other's voices, break down barriers, and create a more inclusive and equitable world for women everywhere.

10. Embracing empowerment and self-expression lead to greater joy, fulfillment, and purpose in women's lives.

Embracing empowerment and self-expression is a transformative journey that can lead to greater joy, fulfillment, and purpose in women's lives. When women assert their power and voice, they reclaim their autonomy and agency, allowing them to pursue their passions and dreams with confidence and conviction. By honoring their authentic selves and expressing their unique perspectives and talents, women experience a deep sense of fulfillment and alignment with their true purpose, fostering a profound sense of inner contentment and satisfaction.

To embark on the journey of empowerment and self-expression, start by reconnecting with your innermost desires, values, and passions. Take the time to reflect on what brings you joy and fulfillment, and identify areas of your life where you feel most alive and authentic. Listen to your intuition and trust your inner wisdom to guide you toward opportunities and experiences that resonate with your deepest aspirations and values.

Cultivate a growth mindset and embrace challenges as opportunities for learning and growth. Recognize that setbacks and obstacles are natural parts of the journey toward empowerment and self-expression, and view them as valuable learning experiences that strengthen your resilience and determination. Embrace failure as a stepping stone to success, and adopt a positive attitude toward experimentation and exploration, knowing that each step forward brings you closer to realizing your full potential.

Surround yourself with supportive individuals who uplift and inspire you to be your best self. Seek out mentors, role models, and peers who share your values and aspirations, and learn from their wisdom, guidance, and experiences. Create a community of like-minded individuals who celebrate your successes, champion your dreams, and provide a safe space for authentic self-expression and growth.

Take inspired action toward your goals and dreams, aligning your thoughts, beliefs, and actions with your vision for a fulfilling and purposeful life. Set meaningful goals that reflect your values and passions, and break them down into manageable steps that you can take each day to move closer to your desired outcomes. Trust in your ability to create the life you envision for yourself, and commit to living authentically and passionately, knowing that you deserve to experience joy, fulfillment, and purpose in every aspect of your life.

About my next book

I hope this book adds immense value to your journey, guiding you toward a life of holistic well-being and fulfillment. Let it be not an end, but a new beginning—a springboard for further exploration and growth. I am thrilled to share that my next endeavor will delve into the fascinating realm of sleep and its profound impact on holistic well-being. Together, we will uncover the secrets of restorative rest, explore the science of sleep, and discover practical strategies for optimizing sleep quality and quantity. Get ready to embark on a journey of rejuvenation and renewal as we unlock the transformative power of sleep for vibrant health and vitality. Stay tuned for an exciting adventure into the world of sleep, where dreams become reality, and every night holds the promise of a brighter tomorrow.

Conclusion

As we reach the peak of our journey through the realms of holistic living for women, let us pause to reflect on the transformative power of this path we've traversed together. Throughout these pages, we've explored the intricate dance of mind, body, and spirit, discovering the profound interconnectedness that shapes our well-being. From nurturing nutrition to invigorating exercise, from the depths of emotional wellness to the heights of spiritual exploration, we've unearthed the keys to unlocking our fullest potential and embracing radiant vitality.

But our journey does not end here; rather, it serves as a springboard for continued growth and evolution. Armed with newfound wisdom and insight, let us stride forward with confidence and conviction, knowing that we possess the tools to craft lives of unparalleled richness and fulfillment. Let us honor our bodies as temples of strength and resilience, our minds as vessels of creativity and clarity, and our spirits as beacons of light and inspiration.

As we bid farewell to these pages, may we carry forth the lessons learned and the insights gained, infusing every moment with intention, purpose, and passion. Let us champion one another on this journey, supporting and uplifting our sisters as they, too, navigate the winding paths of holistic living. And let us embrace the boundless possibilities that await us, knowing that each day brings new opportunities for growth, healing, and joy.

So, dear reader, as you close this book and embark on the next chapter of your life's adventure, do so with an open heart and a courageous spirit. For you are the architect of your destiny, the steward of your well-being, and the master of your fate. May your journey be blessed with abundance, love, and radiant vitality, and may the light of holistic living guide you every step of the way.

www.ingramcontent.com/pod-product-compliance
Lightning Source LLC
Chambersburg PA
CBHW051239130726
47988CB00001B/421